Resist!
Poster Collection
37

Museum für
Gestaltung Zürich

Lars Müller Publishers

1   Käthe Kollwitz
     Nie wieder Krieg
     1924

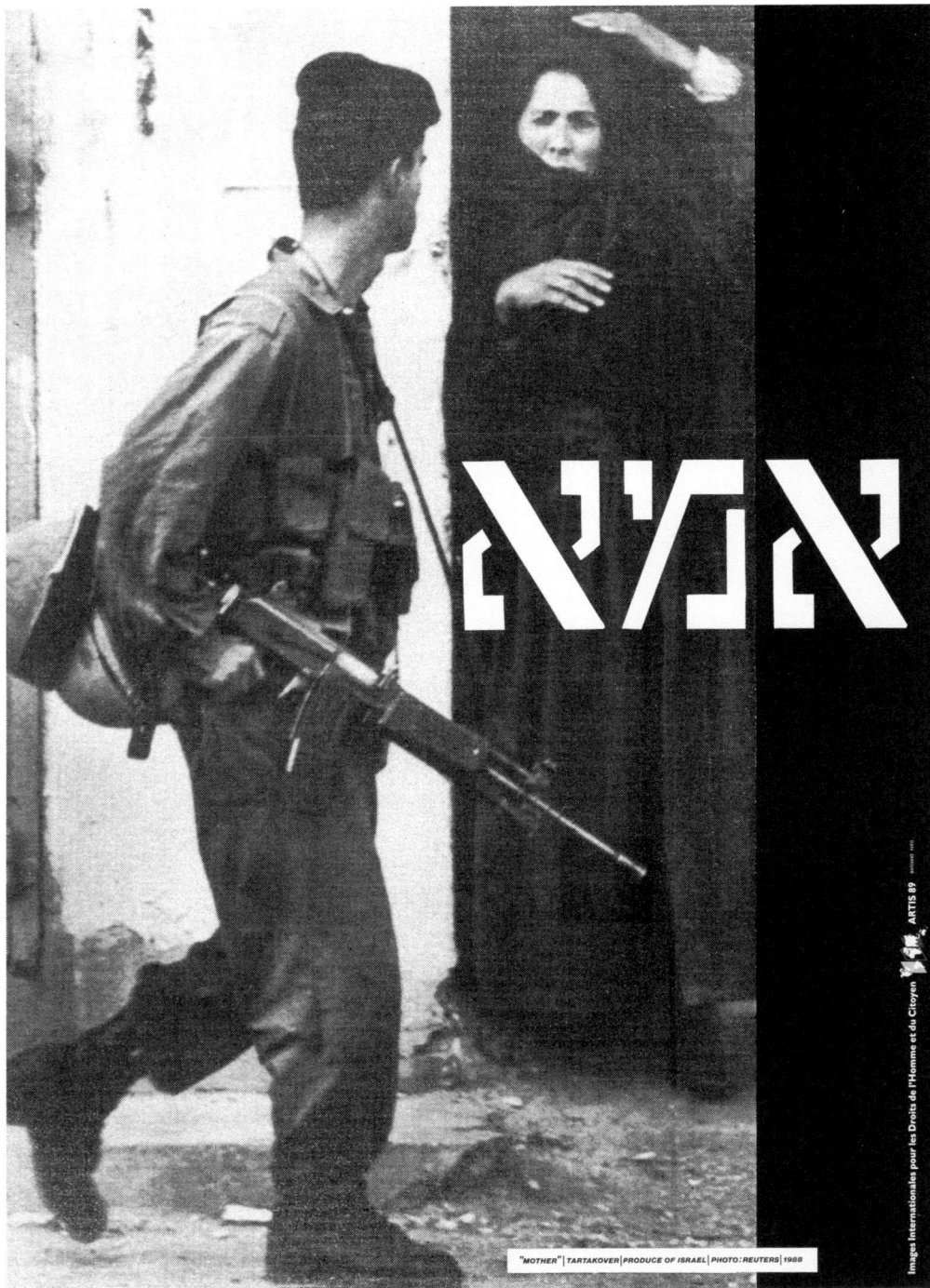

אימא

"MOTHER" | TARTAKOVER | PRODUCE OF ISRAEL | PHOTO : REUTERS | 1988

Images Internationales pour les Droits de l'Homme et du Citoyen   ARTIS 89

2   David Tartakover
"Mother"
1987

5

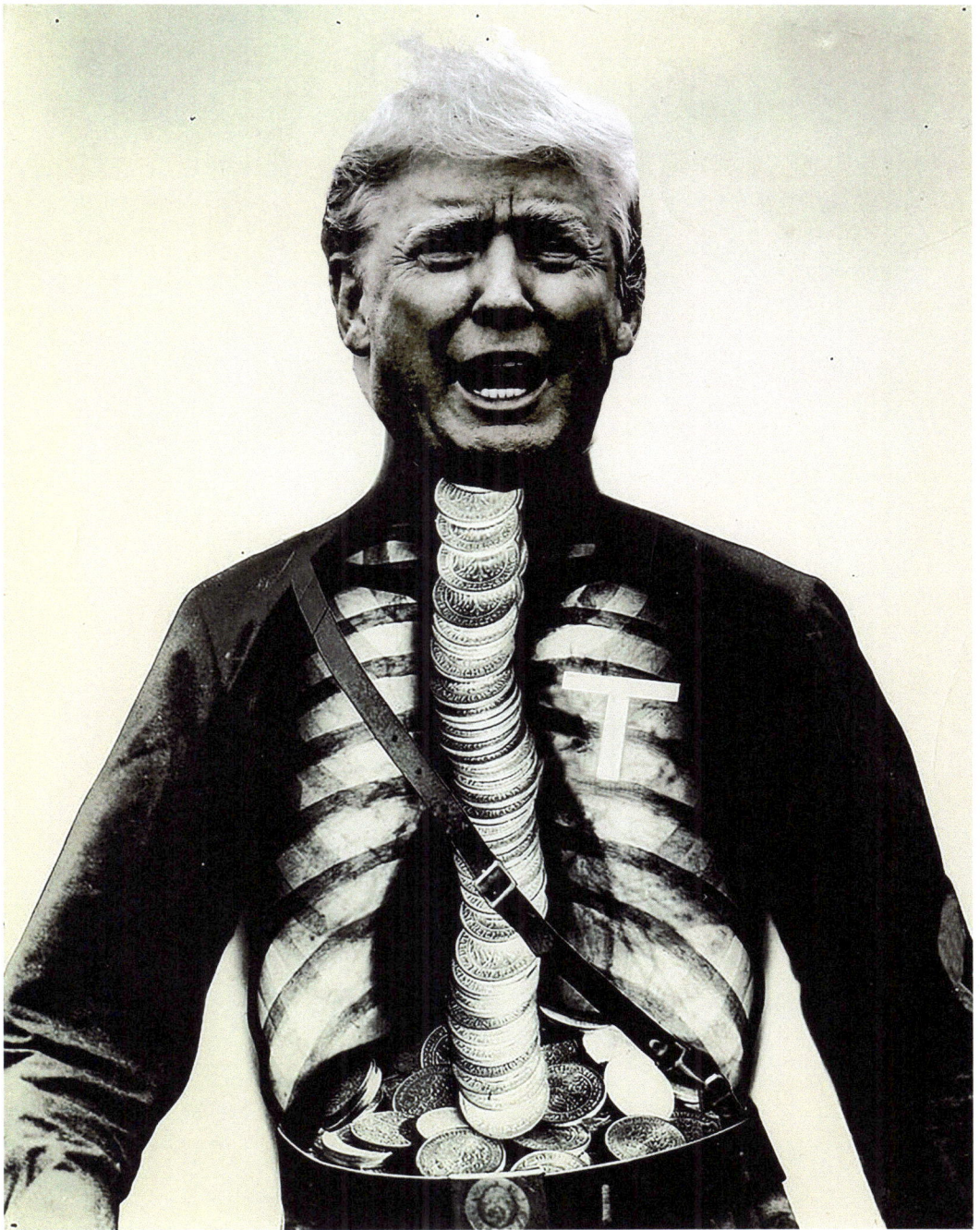

3   Plazm / Joshua Berger, Peter Le
      [ohne Text – no text]
      2016

4 Atelier Populaire
L'ordre règne
1968

Apartheid in Practice

Law & Order in South Africa

The political organisations of the Black majority have been banned and non-racial political organisations are illegal

Leaders of the Black people have been imprisoned, detained, forced into exile or underground activity

During 1976 alone, over 5000 people were detained; many for long periods without trial

All Africans over the age of 15 must carry a pass which controls where they live, work and whether they can travel within the country

During the last 25 years, 11 million Africans have been arrested under the pass laws; on average 1000 are arrested every day

In South Africa, white domination operates in all spheres■Only whites can vote, all members of parliament, all government ministers, all senior civil servants and all judges are white■Apartheid in practice means separate and unequal■This is why apartheid is unpopular, unjust and why the majority oppose it■To enforce apartheid, a battery of security laws exist which enables the government and police to ban organisations, imprison, detain without trial, restrict and ban opponents■When Blacks protest, the police shoot first—as they did in Sharpeville and Soweto

Printed by the Anti-Apartheid Movement, 89 Charlotte Street, London W1, England, in co-operation with United Nations Centre against Apartheid, New York 10017, USA   Design: David King/Proletcult

Twentieth Century Press (1912) Ltd., 8-13 New Inn Street, London EC2A 3HE

5   David King
Apartheid in Practice
1978

SUDAN

6 Luba Lukova
Sudan
1999

Vorwort

Bettina Richter

Das Plakat hat als Medium des Widerstands und des Protests nie an Dringlichkeit verloren, wenngleich es vermehrt nur noch virtuell verbreitet wird. Wird es analog im konsumorientierten, urbanen Raum ausgehängt, ermöglicht es bis heute die partielle Rückeroberung des öffentlichen politischen Diskurses. Die jeweils über Nacht wild plakatierten Anschläge des Atelier Populaire in den Strassen des Pariser Mai 1968 bewiesen dies ebenso wie die Arbeiten des 2006 vor dem Hintergrund politischer Unruhen gegründeten mexikanischen Kollektivs Asamblea de Artistas Revolucionarios de Oaxaca (ASARO), die die Wände in Oaxaca weiterhin sprechen lassen.

Nachdem das Plakat im Ersten Weltkrieg als Propagandamedium entdeckt worden war, eigneten es sich in den 1920er-Jahren auch Kunstschaffende und Gestalterinnen und Gestalter an, um ihr «Nie wieder Krieg!» leidenschaftlich kundzutun. Diese Parole ist heute noch ebenso gültig wie das Aufbegehren gegen den erstarkenden Rechtspopulismus und autokratische Regime. Auch der Kampf für die Rechte von Migrantinnen und Migranten sowie von armutsbetroffenen Menschen weltweit, für die Gleichberechtigung von Frauen, People of Color und queeren Menschen oder für ein radikales Umdenken im Umgang mit unseren Lebensgrundlagen ist von zeitloser, übernationaler Aktualität.

Protestplakate beanspruchen weder unmittelbare Wirksamkeit noch sind sie Ersatz für konkretes Handeln, wohl aber eine Form des politischen Aktivismus. Ihre Berechtigung erhalten sie schon deshalb, weil sie, meist im Eigenauftrag entworfen, für die Gestalterinnen und Gestalter von existenzieller Bedeutung sind. Als oftmals über Kontinente und Zeiten hinweg verständliche Zeichen begleiten sie unterschiedliche Bewegungen und werden so zu einer verbindenden Referenz, klären auf, ermutigen und befördern die internationale Solidarität. Was reaktionäre Mächte so gut zu bedienen wissen, nämlich Affekte, leisten auch Protestplakate: Lachen und Wut finden hier ihren Ausdruck als eigenständige und ermächtigende Widerstandskraft.

Die Publikation zeigt internationale Protestplakate der Plakatsammlung aus rund 100 Jahren. Die individuell oder im Kollektiv arbeitenden Gestalterinnen und Gestalter verbindet ihre emanzipatorische Haltung und die Überzeugung, dass Widerstand einer eigenen Ästhetik bedarf, um nachhaltig und global zu wirken. Visuelle Strategien, bildliche Rhetorik und gestalterische Umsetzung sind vielfältig. Während manche Plakate auf Reflexion abzielen, sprechen andere die Emotionen an. Das Bild der Herrschenden wird demontiert; ihnen stehen Idole gegenüber, die eine bessere Welt versprechen. Dystopische Bilder funktionieren als Provokation und Mahnung, utopische Botschaften halten den Glauben an positive Veränderung wach. Symbole wie die gereckte Faust oder die Taube zeigen ihre ungebrochene Wirkmacht. Subtil und differenziert in der visuellen Argumentation die einen, wirken andere Plakate gerade durch ihre unzweideutige, mitunter brutale Direktheit. Alle jedoch zeugen sie von einem hohen zivilgesellschaftlichen Engagement.

ABOLISH TORTURE

WWW.AMNESTY.ORG

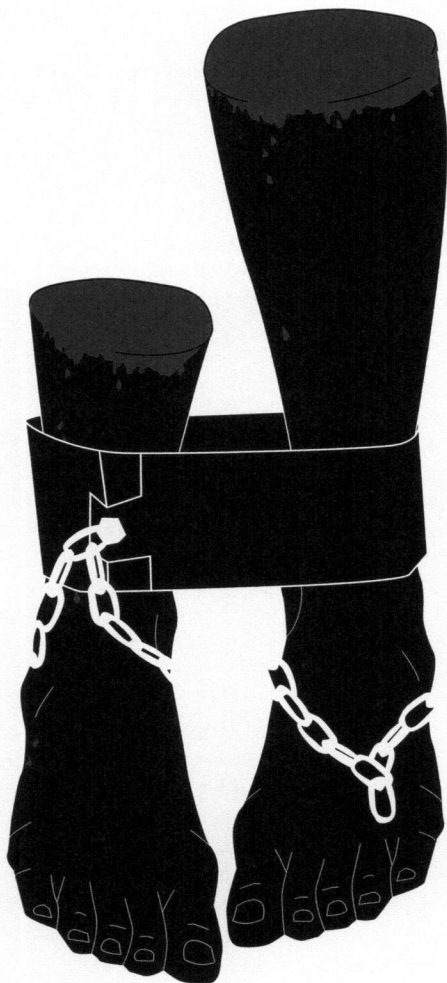

7   Marlena Buczek Smith
Abolish Torture
2007

Even though an increasing number of posters are distributed exclusively in the virtual realm, the poster has lost nothing of its immediacy as a medium of resistance and protest. When posters do appear in analog form in urban consumer spaces, they continue to offer a way to reclaim public political discourse. This potential is evident in the images put up illegally overnight throughout the streets of Paris by the Atelier Populaire in May 1968, as well as in the work of the Mexican collective Asamblea de Artistas Revolucionarios de Oaxaca (ASARO), founded amid political unrest in 2006. Their posters continue to speak to us from the walls of Oaxaca.

After the poster was discovered as a propaganda vehicle during the First World War, artists and designers made use of the medium in the 1920s to fervently proclaim their credo "Never again war!" This slogan remains as relevant today as the fight against the rise of right-wing populism and autocratic regimes. The struggle for migrants' rights, for people affected by poverty worldwide, for equal rights for women, people of color, and queer people, as well as for a radical rethinking of how we use our natural resources – all of these causes have a timeless, transnational relevance.

Protest posters do not claim to have an immediate impact on events, nor are they a substitute for concrete action, but they certainly are an effective form of political activism. Their justification derives from the existential importance they have for their designers, who usually create them on their own initiative. Containing signs and symbols often understood across continents and eras, they accompany popular movements, becoming unifying points of reference. They raise awareness, inspire action, and promote international solidarity. The emotions exploited so deftly by reactionary forces are also tapped by protest posters, in which laughter and anger find expression as independent and empowering forces of resistance.

This publication presents a century of international protest posters from the Poster Collection. Their designers, whether working individually or collectively, share an emancipatory mindset and the conviction that resistance requires its own aesthetic for a sustainable global impact. The examples present diverse visual strategies, pictorial rhetoric, and creative methods. While some posters are designed to make people reflect, others elicit an emotional reaction. The images of those in power are deconstructed and juxtaposed with idols promising a better world. Dystopian images provoke and warn, while utopian messages keep alive the faith in positive change. Symbols such as the raised fist or the dove remain as powerful as ever. While some posters make subtle, nuanced visual arguments, others derive their power from an unambiguous, sometimes brutal, directness. But all testify to a high level of civic engagement.

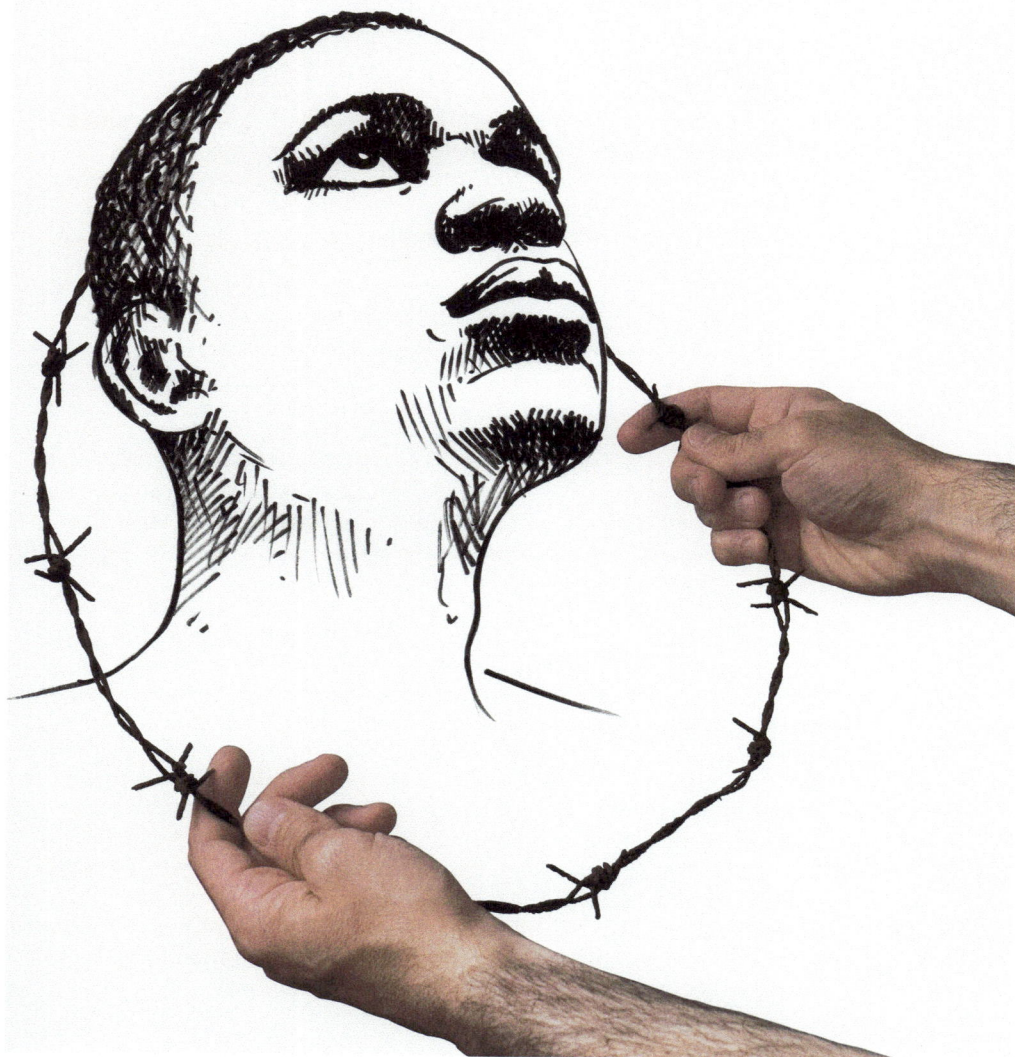

Tomaso Marcolla
Welcome
2011

13

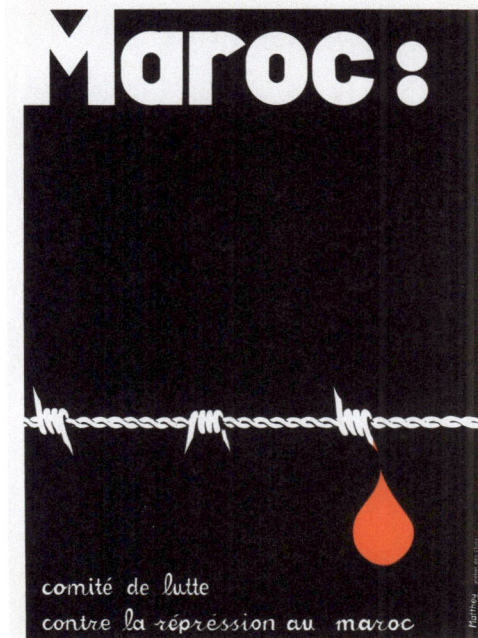

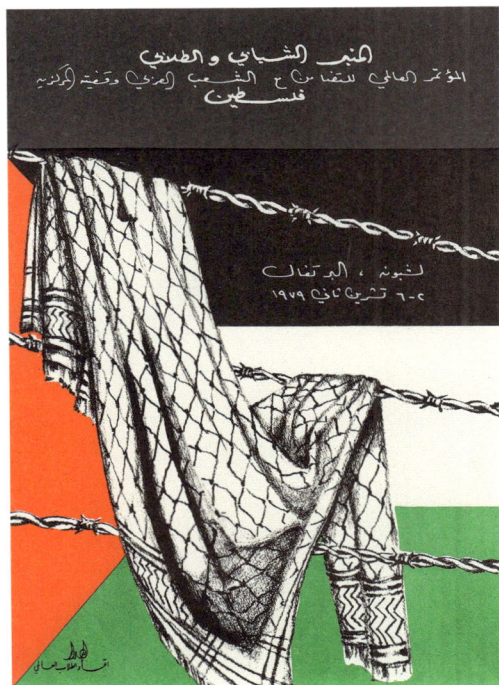

9 Jean-Claude Matthey
Maroc: Comité de lutte contre
la répression au Maroc
ca. 1980

10 Anonym
Internationaler Solidaritätskongress
mit dem arabischen Volk und mit Palästina
1979

11 Ryan Slone
No Other Choice
2016

12 Chaz Maviyane-Davies
Palestine: A Homeland Denied
1980

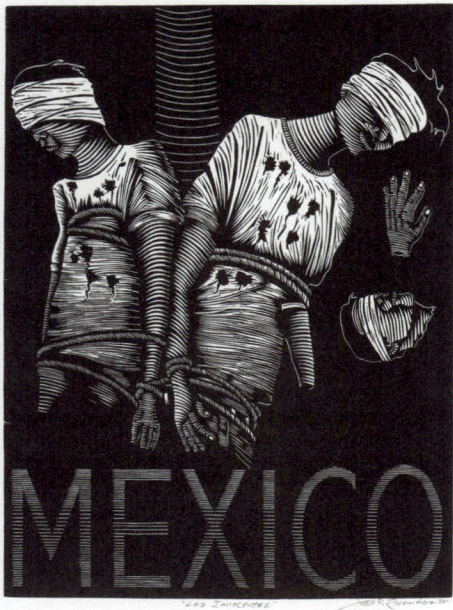

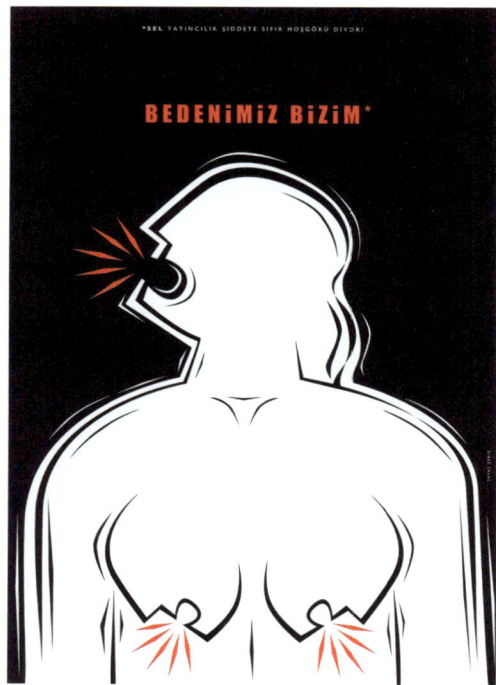

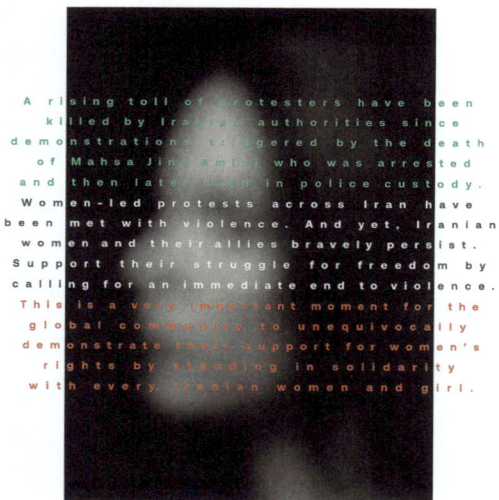

13   Juan R. Fuentes
      Mexico
      2015

14   Goodall Integrated Design / Derwyn Goodall
      A rising toll of protesters have been killed
      by Iranian authorities (…)
      2023

15   Savaş Çekiç
      Bedenimiz bizim
      1998

16   Jeannie Friedman
      Women Unite!
      1976

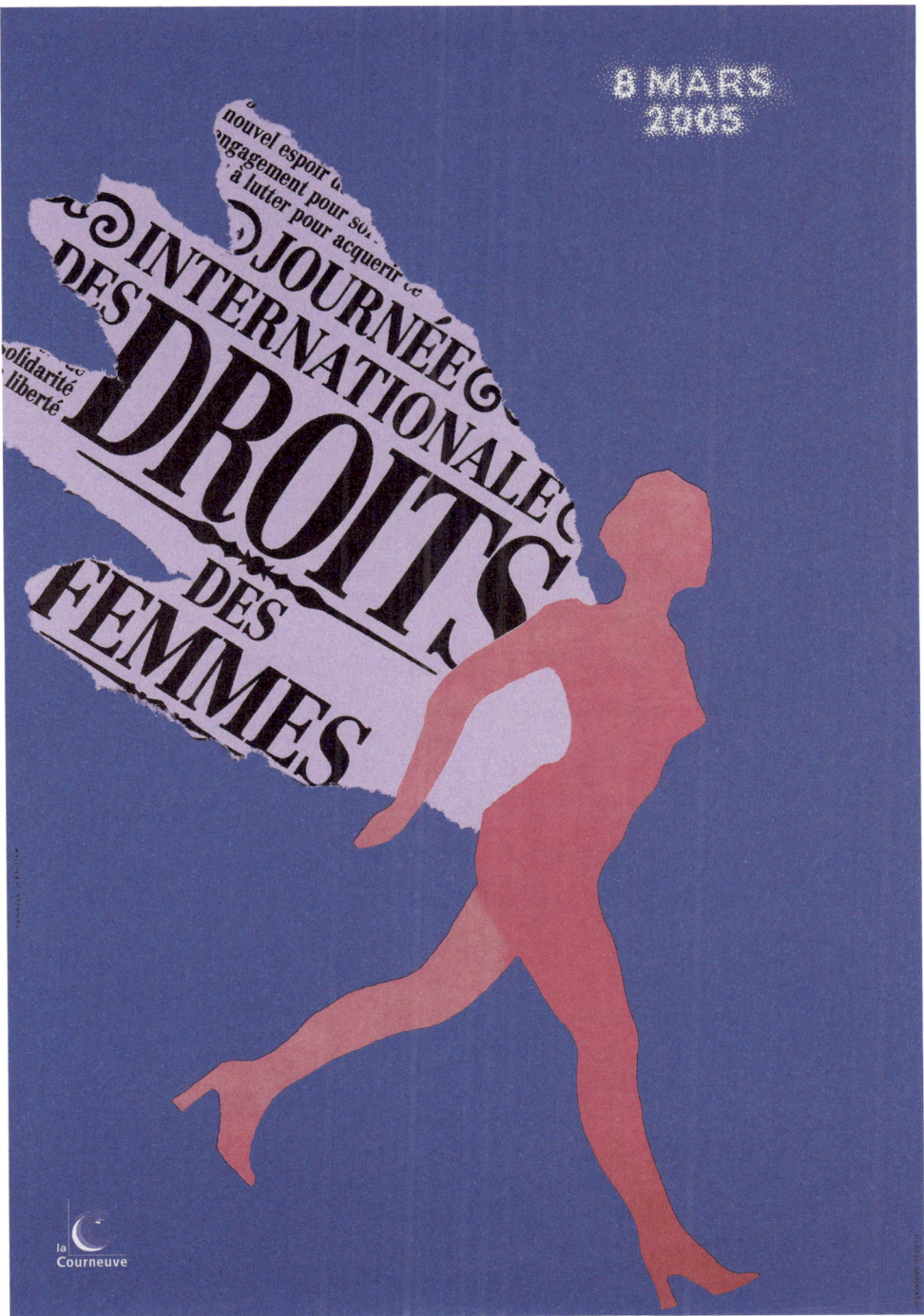

17   Vanessa Vérillon
      Journée internationale
      des droits des femmes
      2005

GUERRILLA GIRLS DEMAND A RETURN TO TRADITIONAL VALUES ON ABORTION.

Before the mid-19th century, abortion in the first few months of pregnancy was legal. Even the Catholic Church did not forbid it until 1869.*

* Carl N. Flanders, *Abortion*, Library in a Book, 1991

A PUBLIC SERVICE MESSAGE FROM GUERRILLA GIRLS 532 LaGuardia Pl. #237, NY 10012

18   Guerrilla Girls
      Guerrilla Girls Demand a Return
      to Traditional Values on Abortion.
      1992

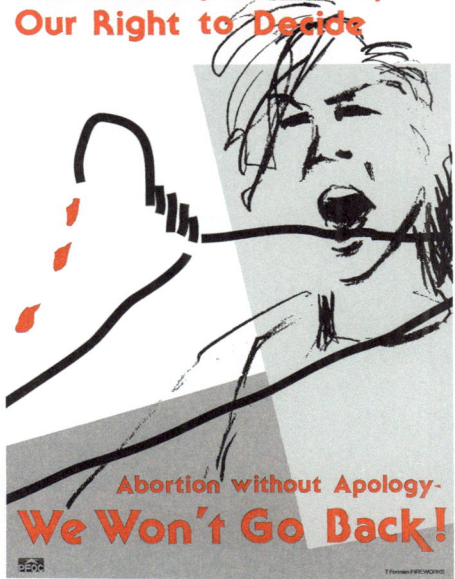

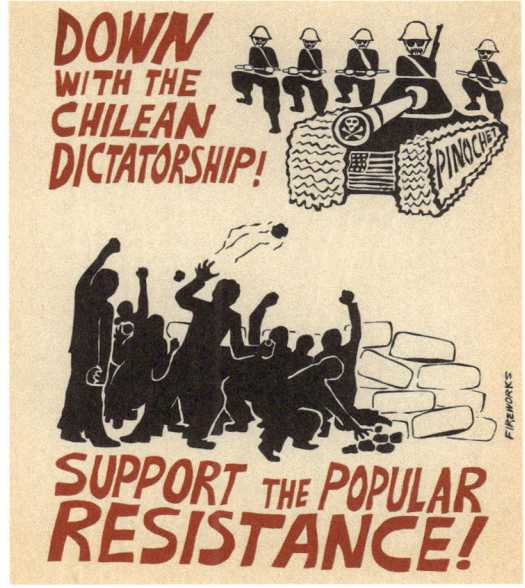

19   Garage Graphix, Talking Posters Project
      I had this big image that I was tough and no-one
      was game to say anything to me about it (…)
      1985

20   Fireworks Graphic Collective / Terry Forman
      Our Bodies, Our Lives, Our Right to Decide
      1989

21   See Red Women's Workshop
      So Long as Women Are Not Free
      the People Are Not Free
      1978

22   Fireworks Graphic Collective / Terry Forman
      Down with the Chilean Dictatorship!
      Support the Popular Resistance!
      1983

CONTRE
LES VIOLENCES
FAITES AUX
FEMMES

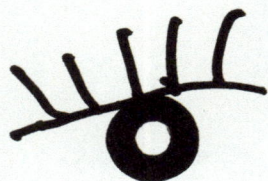

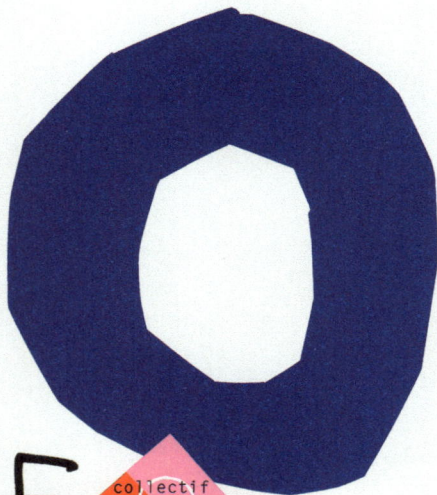

collectif
DROITS
des femmes

21ter rue Voltaire 75011 PARIS
e-mail: colcadac@club-internet.fr
0143 56 3644

23 Atelier de Création Graphique /
    Pierre Bernard, Grégoire Romanet
    Contre les violences faites aux femmes
    2004

24 Gérard Paris-Clavel
Qui a peur d'une femme?
1997

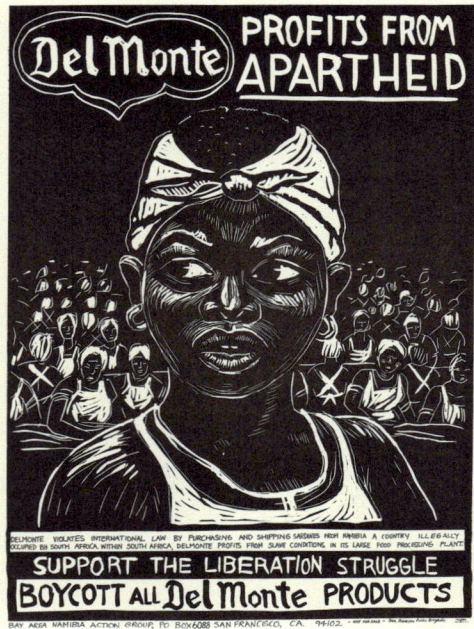

25   Asamblea de Artistas Revolucionarios
      de Oaxaca (ASARO)
      Cuando una mujer avanza ...
      no hay hombre que la detenga
      2007

26   San Francisco Poster Brigade / Rachael Romero
      Stop Forced Sterilization
      1977

27   San Francisco Poster Brigade / Rachael Romero
      Del Monte Profits from Apartheid
      ca. 1977

28   San Francisco Poster Brigade /
      Rachael Romero
      Boycott Nestlé
      1979

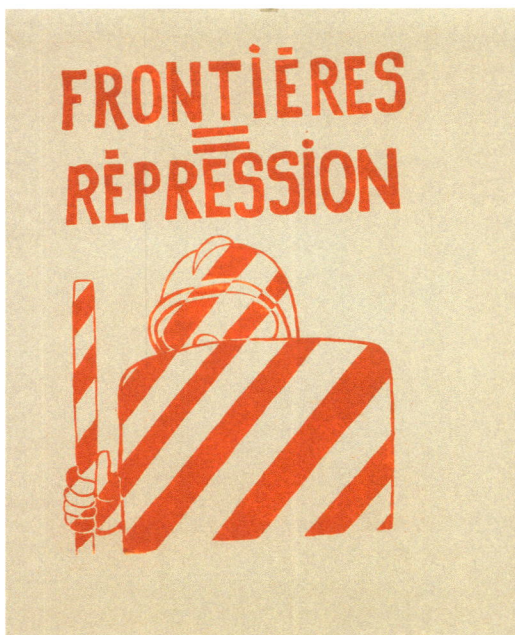

29 Atelier Populaire
Frontières = répression
1968

30 Atelier Populaire
[ohne Text – no text]
1968

31 Atelier Populaire
L'état c'est moi
1968

32 Alain Le Quernec
Attention / Au début Hitler faisait rire
1987

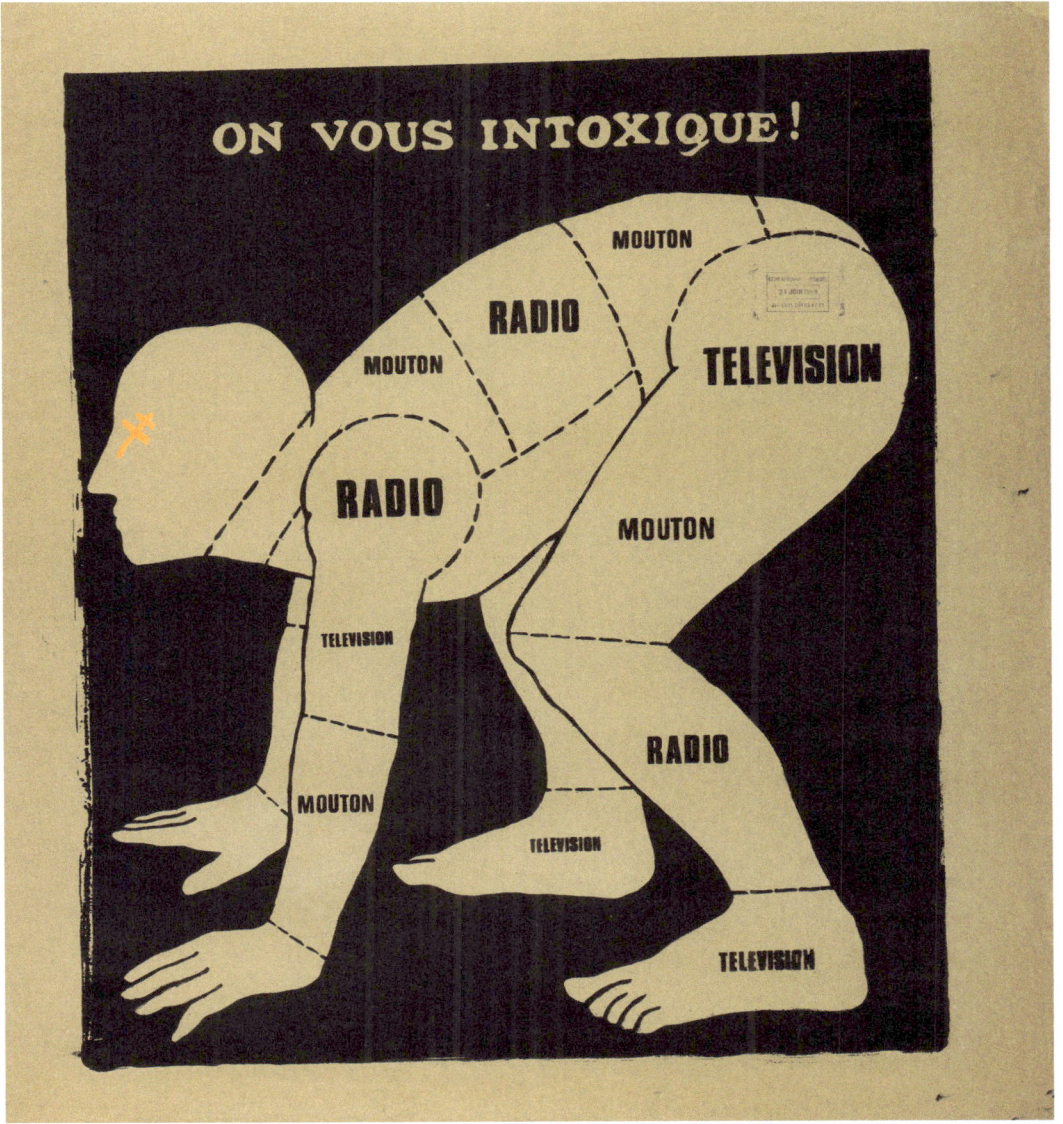

33   Atelier Populaire
     On vous intoxique!
     1968

LA FRANCE ME MÉRITE-T-ELLE ?

Papa et Maman sont des "immigrés".
Moi, je suis né en France, ma langue maternelle est le français.
Bientôt, je vais entrer à la grande école...
Eh bien d'après la loi Pasqua je ne suis pas français !
Qu'est-ce que je suis alors ?
Rien ?
C'est ce qu'on va voir !

34   Nous travaillons ensemble / Alex Jordan
      La France me mérite-t-elle?
      1993

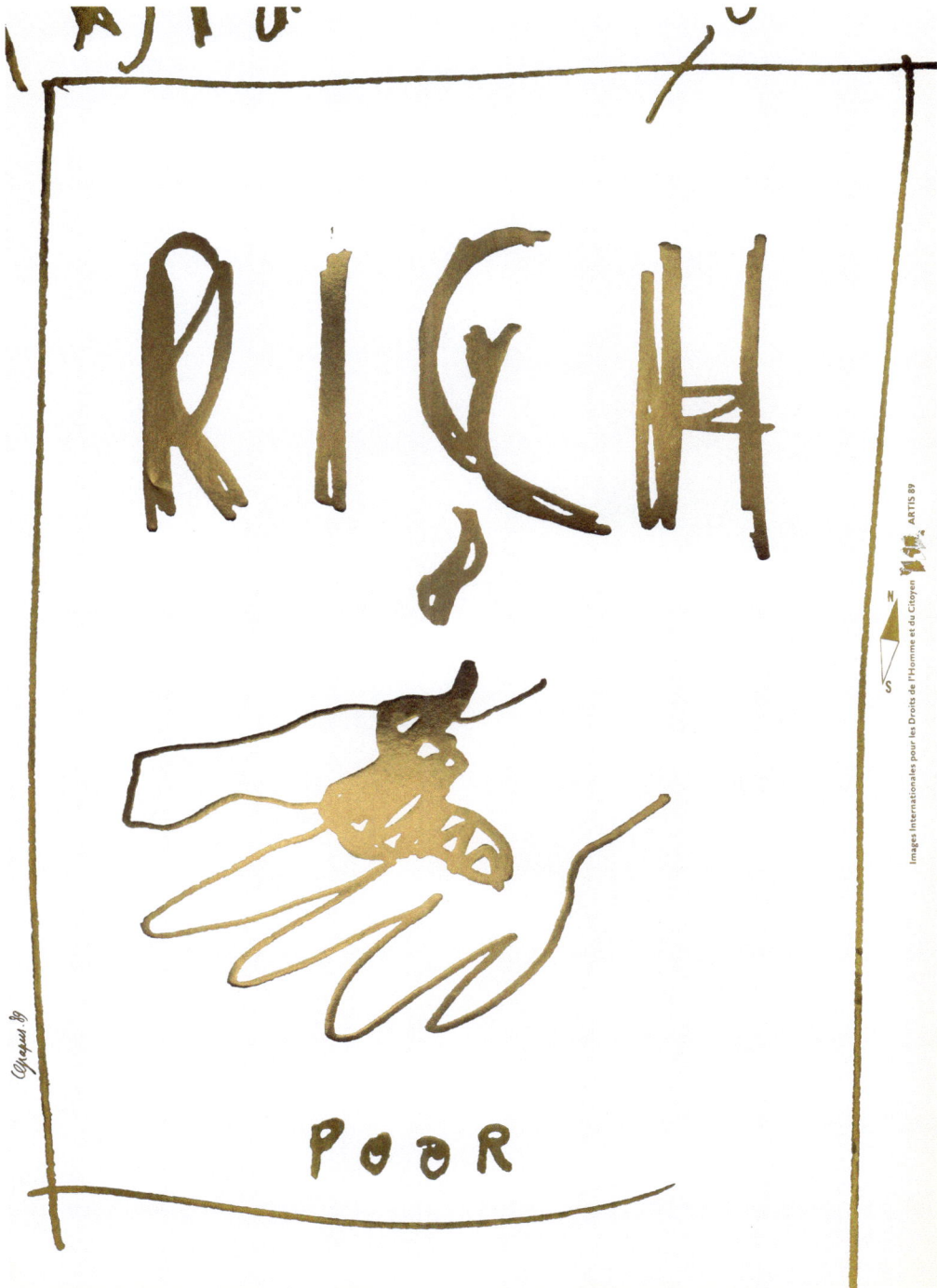

Images Internationales pour les Droits de l'Homme et du Citoyen · ARTS 89

35 Grapus
Rich / Poor
1989

I WANT OUT

36 Larry Dunst
I Want Out
1971

Protest – Plakat – Politik: Das emanzipatorische Plakat gestern und heute

Lisa Bogerts

«Nie wieder Krieg!» Diesen Slogan kennen wir alle. Er steht auf einem Plakat von 1924, das die Künstlerin Käthe Kollwitz für die Sozialistische Arbeiterjugend gestaltete →1. Die geschwungene Handschrift ist genauso simpel, aber dynamisch und stark wie die dazugehörige Zeichnung: Ein junger Mensch reckt leidenschaftlich den Arm in die Luft, mit der Handgeste des Schwurs. Die andere Hand liegt auf seiner Brust, der Mund ist aufgerissen, die Haare wehen nach hinten.

Das heute wohl bekannteste deutsche Antikriegsplakat veranschaulicht, was zur Essenz des emanzipatorischen Protestplakats gehört: Es ist so gestaltet, dass die Botschaft schnell zu verstehen ist. Sowohl Text als auch Bild beunruhigen, empören, aktivieren. Während viele Protestplakate darauf abzielen, die Identifikation mit den Dargestellten zu erwecken oder ein Bewusstsein für ein bestimmtes Thema zu schaffen, erfüllt dieses zusätzlich einen organisatorischen Zweck: Es ruft im öffentlichen Raum dazu auf, an einer Veranstaltung im Rahmen der Massendemonstrationen teilzunehmen, die anlässlich des zehnten Jahrestags des Beginns des Ersten Weltkriegs stattfinden. Der Slogan «Nie wieder!» ist zum geflügelten Wort geworden und wird später von Gestalterinnen und Gestaltern immer wieder aufgegriffen →146/158. Auch heute, 100 Jahre später, ist er noch aktuell.

Sozialwissenschaftlich betrachtet ist Protest ein öffentlich sichtbarer Widerspruch der machtmässig Unterlegenen gegen die Mächtigen und Herrschenden, also vor allem Regierungen oder Wirtschafts eliten. Protest ist partizipative «Politik von unten», die manchmal individuell geäussert, aber meist kollektiv organisiert wird. Emanzipatorische Protestplakate zielen darauf ab, dass sich eine soziale Gruppe aus ihrer Abhängigkeit von einer anderen befreit und gesellschaftlich gleichberechtigt ist.

Plakate sind ein zentrales Medium für die visuelle politische Kommunikation im öffentlichen Raum. Das gilt für solche «von oben» – beauftragt von Regierungen oder erfolgreichen Revolutionsbewegungen[1] – als auch für solche «von unten» – als Ausdrucksmittel von Protest und sozialen Bewegungen.[2] Sie komprimieren Forderungen und Botschaften mithilfe einprägsamer Grafiken und Texte und machen sie damit leichter (be-)greifbar als komplexe politische Manifeste. Protestplakate ermöglichen sowohl kognitive als auch emotionale Zugänge zum Protest: Sie helfen dabei, Fakten und Argumente prägnant zusammenzufassen, aber sie können auch die Empörung, Wut oder Begeisterung auslösen, die Menschen dazu bringen, Forderungen zu unterstützen oder sich Bewegungen sogar anzuschliessen. In der Protest- und Bewegungsforschung gilt als eine der zentralen Mobilisierungstheorien, dass soziale Bewegungen die «kollektive Identität» möglicher Anhängerinnen und Anhänger ansprechen. Visuelle Mittel wie das Plakat können hierfür eine zentrale Rolle spielen, weil sie die emotionale Identifikation mit den emanzipatorischen Subjekten fördern können. Das analoge Protestplakat wird heute oft durch digitale Plakate ersetzt und ruft so zum Beispiel online zur Teilnahme an Demonstrationen oder Petitionen auf. Dennoch verschwinden Protestplakate nicht aus dem (materiellen) öffentlichen Raum und sind weiterhin Teil der visuellen Flut von Botschaften, denen wir täglich auf den Strassen der Städte begegnen.

Die Anfänge des Protestplakats führen bis ins 15. Jahrhundert zurück. Die Erfindung des Buchdrucks mit beweglichen Lettern erlaubt es erstmals in der Geschichte, typografische Druckerzeugnisse maschinell zu vervielfältigen. Martin Luther macht 1517 seinen Protest gegen den Ablasshandel der katholischen Kirche öffentlich, indem er seine 95 Thesen für alle sichtbar an der Schlosskirche in Wittenberg anbringt. Im 19. Jahrhundert ermöglicht das Druckverfahren der Lithografie dann, farbige Bildplakate industriell herzustellen.[3] Neben der Erfindung der dampfbetriebenen Papierherstellung trägt dies dazu bei, dass Plakate als Medium der Massenkommunikation erschwinglich und populär werden und sich schnell und massenhaft verbreiten lassen.

Seine Hochzeit erlebt das politische Bildplakat im 20. Jahrhundert. Visuelle Kommunikation findet grösstenteils noch analog statt und ist nicht so stark in den digitalen Raum verlagert wie im 21. Jahrhundert. Die Frauenbewegung bringt 1909 in London das Suffrage Atelier hervor. Das Künstlerinnenkollektiv bildet Frauen in Drucktechniken fort und ermutigt sie dazu, Grafiken für die politischen Kampagnen der Suffragetten zu entwerfen, die schliesslich 1918 das Wahlrecht für Frauen in Grossbritannien erwirken.[4]

Zeitgleich stellen erfolgreiche sozialistische Revolutionärinnen und Revolutionäre die bildende Kunst in ihre Dienste und fördern somit avantgardistische Strömungen. Dazu gehören etwa der mexikanische Muralismus, der malerisch-illustrativ die marginalisierte indigene Bevölkerung sowie Arbeiterinnen und Arbeiter sichtbar macht, oder der russische Konstruktivismus, der mit dem Fokus auf Fotografie und Typografie das Grafikdesign der Moderne einleitet und schwarz-rot-weiss als emblematische «linke» Farbkombination etabliert. Sie prägen damit die diversen Protestästhetiken des 20. Jahrhunderts, auch wenn es sich bei den von Regierungen beauftragten Plakaten keinesfalls um Protest «von unten» handelt.[5]

In der historischen Betrachtung erweist sich das Plakat in der Zwischenkriegszeit als immer bedeutsameres politisches Kommunikationsmedium. Vor der nationalsozialistischen Machtübernahme nutzt John Heartfield die Fotomontage, um sich über Adolf Hitler lächerlich zu machen. Das Plakat «Adolf, der Übermensch: Schluckt Gold und redet Blech» wird während des Reichstagwahlkampfes 1932 grossformatig gehängt. Es demonstriert, dass auch Humor und Satire dazu dienen können, um sich über die Machthabenden lustig zu machen und damit ein empowerndes Moment bei ihren Gegnerinnen und Gegnern zu erzeugen →127. Die Demontage von Politikerinnen und Politikern, Diktatorinnen und Diktatoren wird bis heute als Bildstrategie konsequent weitergeführt.

Die Bildsprache des heissen Pariser Mai 1968 wird geprägt durch die Plakate des Atelier Populaire. Obwohl – oder gerade weil – die Siebdrucktechnik rudimentär ist und der Zeitdruck des Strassenkampfs auch einmal zu schief gedruckten Motiven führt, haben sich die zahlreichen Aushänge ins kollektive visuelle Gedächtnis eingebrannt →70. Die auf einem Plakat dargestellte Gruppe von Arbeitern mit erhobener Faust und Werkzeug gehört zu den häufigsten politischen Symbolen transnationaler Protestästhetik. Die in der besetzten Druckwerkstatt der École des Beaux-Arts entstandenen Plakate repräsentieren in ihrer minimalistischen Technik und DIY-Ästhetik authentisch die dahinterstehende Bewegung und ihre Ziele. Sie sind schnell und kostengünstig produzierbar, sodass Plakatmobilisierung nicht nur Gruppen mit Geld oder hochwertigem Equipment vorbehalten ist. Zudem wirken sie dort, wo das Protestplakat hingehört – nämlich im öffentlichen Raum, auf der Strasse, und nicht (nur) im geschützten Raum von Kunst- und Kulturinstitutionen.

1968 ist auch das Jahr, in dem mit Martin Luther King eine Ikone des gewalt-
freien Teils der US-amerikanischen Bürgerrechtsbewegung ermordet wird.
Sein Porträt auf Plakaten →163 zeigt ebenso wie jenes von Angela Davis →104,
wie sehr die massenhafte Darstellung charismatischer Persönlichkeiten
dazu beitragen kann, dass sich Anhängerinnen und Anhänger mit einer Protestbewegung identifizieren. Davis repräsentiert den radikaleren Arm
der Bewegung und pflegt enge Verbindungen zur Black Panther Party. Deren
«Kulturminister» Emory Douglas gestaltet zahlreiche Plakate mit starker
Farb- und Formensprache, die – oft bewaffnete – Schwarze Aktivistinnen
oder Aktivisten in selbstbewusster Pose darstellen.[6] Hier zeigt sich beispielhaft, wie wichtig es für eine marginalisierte Gruppe ist, sich im öffentlichen (visuellen) Diskurs trotz struktureller Nachteile selbst repräsentieren
zu können, jenseits von Opferklischees.

Während dieser rhetorische Ansatz der Heroisierung von Widerstands-
kämpferinnen und -kämpfern mobilisieren will, zielen andere Protestplakate
darauf ab, Empathie zu wecken. Das Plakat «Eat» von Tomi Ungerer etwa
steht emblematisch für grafischen Protest gegen den Vietnamkrieg und die
künstlerische Nord-Süd-Solidarität →39. Es erzielt seine einprägsame und
unbehagliche Wirkung wohl auch dadurch, dass es «die Anderen» (die Viet-
namesinnen und Vietnamesen) als Opfer darstellt. Der Anblick ihres Leids
löst bei den Betrachtenden Unbehagen aus, veranschaulicht aber auch die
Gefahr, mit ihrer klischeehaften Darstellung rassistische Stereotype zu
reproduzieren.[7]

Im Sinne der Süd-Süd-Solidarität rufen viele Plakate aus Kuba zu Befreiungskämpfen auf, unter anderem zur Unterstützung von Vietnam, Kambodscha und Laos gegen den US-Imperialismus →88. Die internationalistische
Organisation für Solidarität mit den Völkern in Asien, Afrika und Lateinamerika (OSPAAAL) beauftragt 1968 die Grafikerin Asela Maria Pérez mit der
Gestaltung eines Plakats zum internationalen Tag der Solidarität mit Lateinamerika →65. Der Offsetdruck stellt die Landfläche Südamerikas als rote
Faust dar – dem wohl häufigsten linken Protestsymbol –, die ein Gewehr er-
greift, und sendet somit unmissverständliche Signale an mögliche Invasoren.[8]

Dennoch sind im Globalen Norden entstandene Solidaritätsplakate in euro-
päischen Sammlungen häufiger vertreten als solche der betroffenen Grup-
pen selbst. Das Grafikkollektiv Fireworks, in Los Angeles und San Francisco
aktiv, drückt seine Solidarität mit dem chilenischen Widerstand gegen
Augusto Pinochet in einem Plakat von 1983 aus: «Down with the Chilean
Dictatorship! Support the Popular Resistance!» →22. In Anlehnung an den
Stil des Atelier Populaire stellt der Siebdruck in den typisch sozialistischen
Farben Rot, Schwarz und Weiss das archaische Bild des antagonistischen
Strassenkampfes aus der Perspektive der chilenischen Widerstandskämpfer
gegen die Panzer des Diktators dar.

Ende der 1970er- und Anfang der 1980er-Jahre macht die Frauenbewegung
durch ganz unterschiedliche Plakat-Rhetoriken auf sich aufmerksam. Die
Guerrilla Girls prangern den Sexismus in der Kunstwelt und der Gesellschaft
an, indem sie Fakten mit deftiger Ironie präsentieren und die Öffentlichkeit
auf humoristische Weise aufzuklären versuchen →18. Eine andere Strategie ist
die Darstellung von Schmerz und körperlichem Leid, die prinzipiell alle
Menschen nachempfinden können, unabhängig von ihren politischen Ansich-
ten. Die Mimik der Frauen auf Jeannie Friedmans Plakat «Women Unite!» →16
oder auf dem des Grafikkollektivs Fireworks →20 kann sowohl als Ausdruck
kämpferischer Wut als auch als Ausdruck von Schmerz gelesen werden.
Bei Letzterem lässt der Blut tropfende Drahtkleiderbügel jedoch förmlich den
körperlichen Schmerz nachempfinden, den Frauen erleiden, wenn sie durch

ein Abtreibungsverbot auf provisorische, nicht-medizinische Methoden zurückgreifen müssen. In der Türkei werden für die Kampagne «Unsere Körper gehören uns – Nein zum sexuellen Missbrauch!» ebenfalls Plakate produziert, die den
körperlichen und seelischen Schmerz der Frau darstellen, mit einem Fokus
auf die Rechte von Sexarbeiterinnen →15.

Dass Plakate auch im Kontext von internationalen politischen Kampagnen
entstehen, zeigen die Auftragsarbeiten für grosse Nichtregierungsorganisationen
wie Amnesty International →95.[9] Das Kampagnenmaterial ist meist online zum
Download verfügbar, um es für den eigenen, lokalen Protest auf der Strasse zu
verwenden. Umgekehrt regen auch weniger strategisch organisierte, sondern
dezentrale und sich organisch im Netz entwickelnde Bewegungen Grafikerinnen
und Grafiker dazu an, sich mit Plakaten für ihre Ziele einzusetzen. Dazu gehört
die 2017 entstehende #MeToo-Bewegung, deren enorme Reichweite unter anderem vom Grafiker Lahav Halevy typografisch veranschaulicht wird →133. Eine
ähnliche rein typografisch erzeugte räumliche Wirkung hat ein Plakat zu den Frau-
enprotesten im Iran, die 2022 durch den gewaltsamen Tod von Jina Mahsa
Amini losgetreten werden: Das Studio der in Berlin lebenden Exil-Iranerin Golnar
Kat Rahmani wählt eine dynamische Darstellung des Slogans «Zan, Zendegi,
Āzādī» (Frau, Leben, Freiheit), um auf Persisch die iranische Diasporagemein-
schaft anzusprechen →137.

Insbesondere die Protestbewegungen im Nahen und Mittleren Osten nutzen
während des Arabischen Frühlings in den 2010er-Jahren hauptsächlich digitale
Mobilisierungskanäle und Bilder auf Social Media, um sich zu koordinieren
und zu mobilisieren. Ausschliesslich online verbreitete Plakate aus dem zivilgesellschaftlichen Aufstand in Syrien, wie die des anonymen Kollektivs Alshaab
Alsori Aref Tarekh (Das syrische Volk kennt seinen Weg), zeigen, dass Plakate im
Netz auch dann zum Strassenprotest aufrufen können, wenn ihr Aushang
auf der Strasse selbst zu gefährlich ist.[10] Dennoch veranschaulichen Begriffe
wie «Social Media Wall», dass digitale Bilder auch im digitalen Raum noch
immer an einer «Wand» angebracht werden.

Thematisch decken die Protestgrafiken sozialer Bewegungen ab den 2000er-
Jahren eine grosse Bandbreite ab, die von Flucht und Migration →55/139 über den
Klimaschutz →73 bis zur Ehrung von Women of Color als emanzipatorische
Vorreiterinnen →91/121 reicht. Als Teil der Serie Celebrate People's History der
Justseeds Artists' Cooperative entsteht 2020 ein Plakat der brasilianischen
Gestalterin Camila Rosa →125. Anhand dieses Beispiels lässt sich abschliessend
noch einmal zusammenfassen, was die transnationale Wirkung des emanzi-
patorischen Protestplakats ausmacht: Es informiert über soziale und politische
Widerstandsbewegungen wie hier über die des Movimento dos Trabalhadores
Sem Terra (MST), eine der grössten lateinamerikanischen Bewegungen. Gleichzeitig bietet es Identifikationsfiguren, die in ästhetisch ansprechender und
gleichzeitig kämpferischer Weise eine empowernde Wirkung haben können.
Das Plakat appelliert sowohl auf kognitiver Ebene, durch logische Argumente,
als auch auf emotionaler Ebene, durch die dargestellten Frauen, ihre teils
wütende Mimik und die erhobene Faust. Genau wie der Protest selbst kann emanzipatorische Gestaltung das Gefühl kollektiver Identität, die Zugehörigkeit zu
einer Gemeinschaft bekräftigen. Protestplakate können eine Bewegung sowohl
nach innen in ihrer Kohäsion stärken als auch nach aussen wirken, indem
sie soziale Gruppen und ihre Forderungen im öffentlichen Raum und somit im
öffentlichen Diskurs sichtbar machen – heute genau wie schon vor 100 Jahren.

1   David King, *Russian Revolutionary Posters. From Civil War to Socialist Realism, from Bolshevism to the End of Stalinism*, London 2015.

2   Lisa Bogerts, *The Aesthetics of Rule and Resistance. Analyzing Political Street Art in Latin America*, New York 2022.

3   Bettina Richter, «Von Pasquino zu Anonymous», in: Basil Rogger, Jonas Voegeli, Ruedi Widmer und Museum für Gestaltung Zürich (Hg.), *Protest. Eine Zukunftspraxis*, Zürich 2018, S. 378–380.

4   Liz McQuiston, *Protest! A History of Social and Political Protest Graphics*, London 2019, S. 42–49; Gerda Breuer, «Suffragetten: Frühes Corporate Design und Kommunikationsdesign in England», in: dies., *HerStories in Graphic Design: Dialoge, Kontinuitäten, Selbstermächtigungen. Grafikdesignerinnen 1880 bis heute*, Berlin 2023, S. 102–113.

5   Bogerts 2022 (Anm. 2).

6   https://collections.library.yale.edu/catalog/33215778.

7   McQuiston 2019 (Anm. 4), S. 100.

8   Richard Frick, *Das trikontinentale Solidaritätsplakat*, Bern 2003.

9   Amnesty International, Joanne Rippon, *The Art of Protest. A Visual History of Dissent and Resistance*, Woodbridge 2019.

10 www.britishmuseum.org/collection/term/BIOG246525.

JOIN THE FREE AND FAT

37   Tomi Ungerer
Join the Free and Fat Society
1967

OCIETY

Victore Design Works / James Victore
Disney Go Home
ca. 1997

35

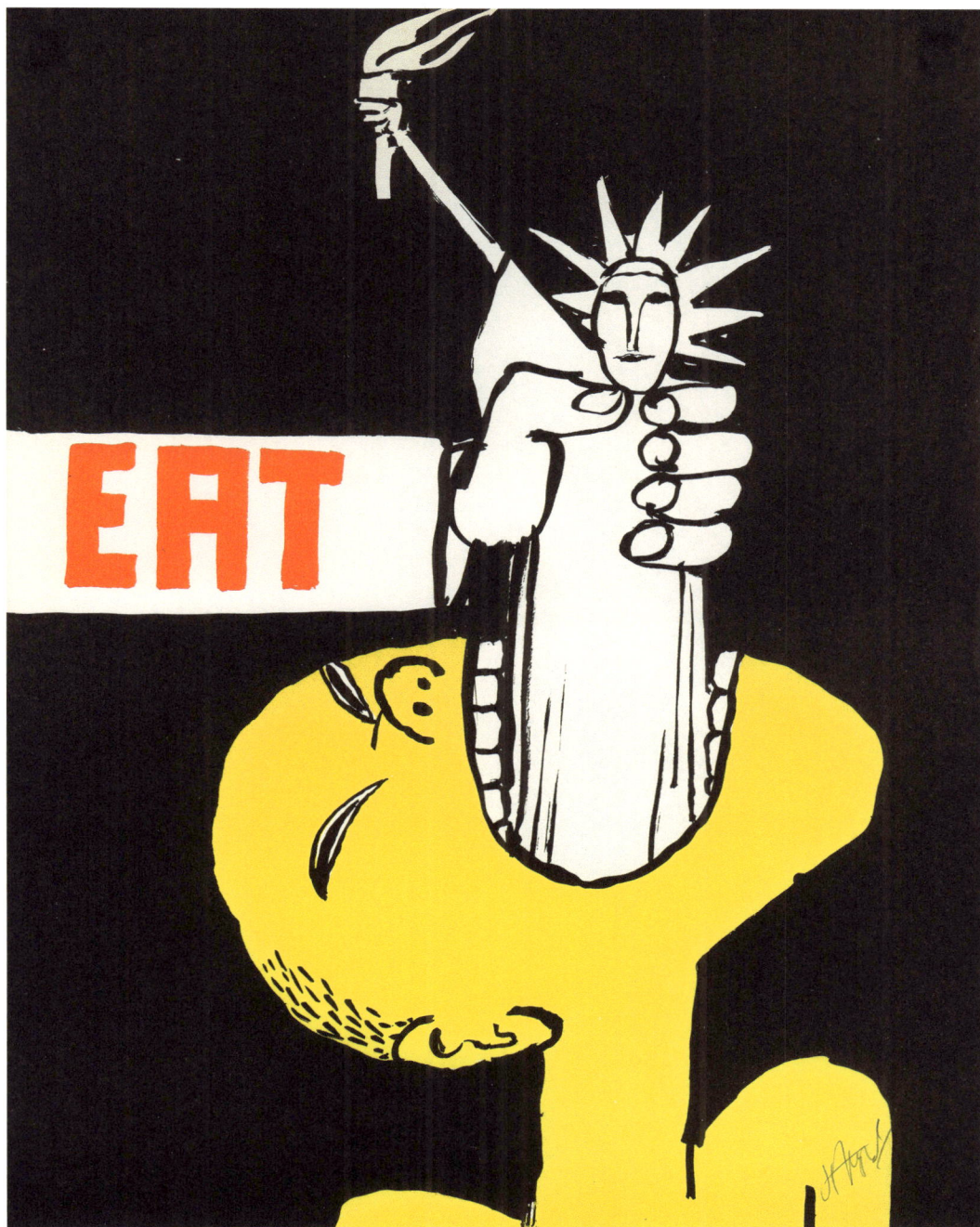

39   Tomi Ungerer
      Eat
      1967

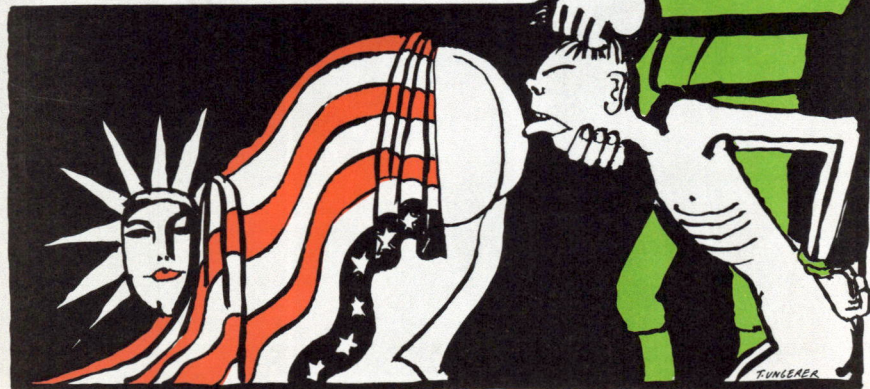

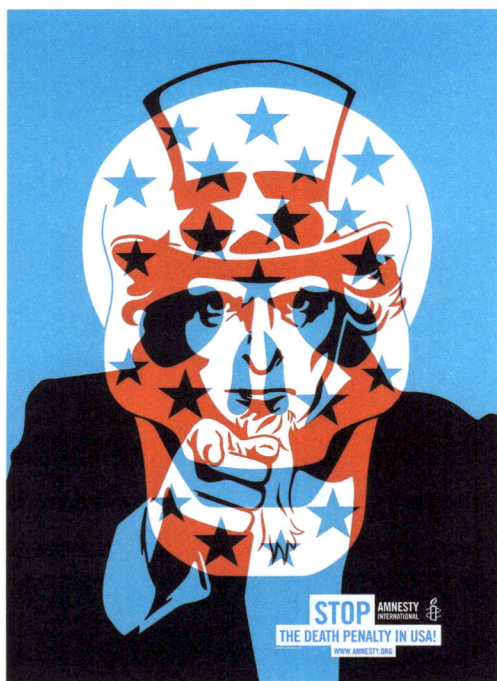

40   Tomi Ungerer
       Kiss for Peace
       1967

41   Fons Hickmann m23 / Fons Hickmann
       Stop the Death Penalty in USA!
       2010

Made in America: Eine US-amerikanische Sichtweise auf Protestplakate

Silas Munro

Protest ist ein altbekanntes Thema in der Geschichte der Vereinigten Staaten. In einer Endlosschleife drückt sich darin Widerstand gegen Tyrannei aus. Inmitten des drastischen Wandels unter Präsident Donald Trump in den ersten Monaten seiner zweiten Amtszeit 2025 ist das Protestplakat ebenso Teil der Gegenwart wie der Vergangenheit. Kürzlich beteiligten sich Hundert-tausende Amerikanerinnen und Amerikaner unter dem Motto «Hands Off» (Hände weg) in grossen und kleinen Städten im ganzen Land an Demonstra-tionen, um gegen die Abschaffung zahlreicher Regierungsprogramme zu protestieren. Dieser Moment erinnert mich an den ersten Kurs in Designge-schichte, den ich als 19-jähriger Student besuchte. In seiner Vorlesung über Nazi-Propaganda zeigte Douglas Scott das Hitler-Plakat von John Heart-field: In einer meisterhaften frühen Fotomontage hatte er eine schauder-hafte Darstellung des Diktators als lebender Leichnam geschaffen, aus des-sen Speiseröhre als Symbol seiner Gier Goldmünzen herausquellen →127. Die moderne Interpretation des Bildes von Plazm aus dem Jahr 2016, auf der Donald Trump anstelle von Hitler zu sehen ist, wirkt nun wie eine furchter-regende Prophezeiung →3.

Visuelle Gegenkultur und aktivistischer Protest gehen in der Geschichte der amerikanischen Jugendkultur Hand in Hand. Plakate als Mittel des Widerstands widersetzten sich der rassistischen Diskriminierung und for-derten Bürgerrechte ein, etwa die des Student Nonviolent Coordinating Committee, der AfriCOBRA-Bewegung oder der Black Panther Party. Diese von Afroamerikanerinnen und Afroamerikanern angeführten Designbe-wegungen kämpften gegen die Segregation und prägten gleichzeitig eine Schwarze Ästhetik, inspiriert sowohl von afrikanischer Kunst als auch von zeitsparenden, kostengünstigen Lo-Fi-Produktionstechniken, wie sie Emory Douglas bei seinen Druckbuchstaben und Illustrationen einsetzte. In der Plakatsammlung des Museum für Gestaltung Zürich sind solche Plakate nicht vertreten, was die lange Geschichte der rassistischen Diskriminierung in den USA und Europa bezeugt, die ihre Wurzeln im transatlantischen Sklavenhandel hat. Hingegen umfasst die Sammlung Solidaritätsplakate von Bürgerrechts- und Antikriegsbewegungen, beispielsweise Plakate gegen den Vietnamkrieg, die oftmals von Kollektiven stammen.

Design Is Play / Mark Fox, Angie Wang
Trump
2016

American Made:
A U.S. View of
the Protest Poster

Silas Munro

Protest is a well-worn subject in the history of the United States. In an endless loop, it expresses defiance against tyranny. Amidst a drastic shift in the U.S. government led by President Donald Trump during the early months of his second term in 2025, the protest poster is as much a part of the present as it is of the past. Recently, hundreds of thousands of Americans across the country participated in "hands-off" demonstrations in cities large and small, critiquing the dismantling of numerous government programs. This moment brings me back to the first lecture course on design history that I took as a 19-year-old design student. In his lecture on Nazi propaganda, Douglas Scott showed John Heartfield's poster of Hitler, which masterfully employs early photomontage techniques to create a chilling depiction of the dictator as a living cadaver, his greed symbolized by gold coins spilling from his esophagus →127. The image's modern reinterpretation, featuring Donald Trump in Hitler's place and designed by Plazm in 2016, now seems eerily prophetic →3.

Countercultural visual history and activist protest go hand in hand in the American youth culture tradition. Posters operate as tools of resistance in support of racial integration and civil rights in graphics produced by the Student Nonviolent Coordinating Committee, the AfriCOBRA movement, and the printed materials of the Black Panther Party. These Black American-led design movements fought segregation while simultaneously defining a Black aesthetic, inspired both by African art and time-efficient and cost-effective lo-fi production techniques like Emory Douglas's use of press type lettering and illustrations. These posters are not represented in the Poster Collection of the Museum für Gestaltung Zürich, reflecting the deep histories of discrimination in the United States and Europe that date back to their participation in the transatlantic slave trade. The collection features solidarity posters from civil rights and anti-war movements, exemplified by anti-Vietnam War posters that often came from collectives.

NON AUX ESSAIS

NUCLÉAIRES

Gauguin et U.G.Sato

image réalisée par l'association de graphistes japonais " Jagda ", 1995

43   U. G. Sato
Non aux essais nucléaires
1995

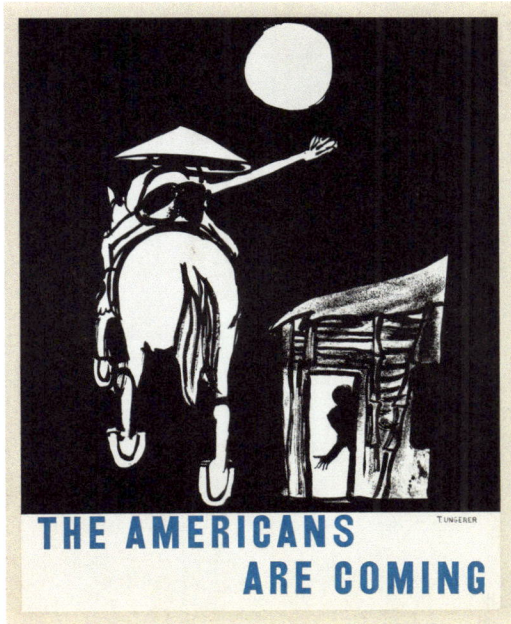

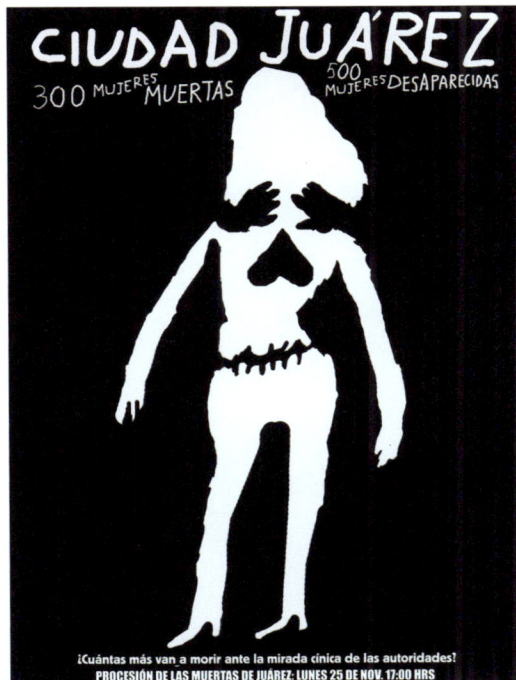

44 Tomi Ungerer
    The Americans Are Coming
    1967

45 Alejandro Magallanes
    Ciudad Juárez
    2003

46 Pedro Yamashita
    Peace
    2001

47 Victore Design Works / James Victore
    Racism and the Death Penalty
    1993

48 Anonym
[ohne Text – no text]
ca. 1973

49   Niklaus Troxler
     [Tote Bäume]
     1992

50   Luba Lukova
      Eco Crime
      1999

51   Victore Design Works / James Victore
      25 Years / Earth Day / 1970–1995
      1995

52   Asamblea de Artistas Revolucionarios
      de Oaxaca (ASARO)
      Reformas energetica educativa
      financiera electoral laboral
      2015

53   Elisabetta Carboni
      Lavoratori, lavoratrici, studenti, sosteniamo
      con la nostra presenza i pescatori di Cabras
      ingiustamente processati
      1972

54 Piär Amrein
Mehr für die Reichen / Meer für die Armen
2015

55 Götz Gramlich, Klaus Staeck
[ohne Text – no text]
2014

Protest – Posters – Politics: The Emancipatory Poster Then and Now

Lisa Bogerts

"Never again war!" is a slogan we all know well. It appeared in 1924 on a poster designed by the artist Käthe Kollwitz for the Socialist Workers' Youth League in Germany →1. The dynamic handwriting is simple yet powerful, just like the accompanying drawing, which shows a young person energetically raising their arm straight into the air in an oath. The other hand is on their heart, their mouth wide open, their hair blown back.

What is arguably the best-known German anti-war poster illustrates the essential features of any emancipatory protest poster: it is designed to be understood quickly, and both text and image provoke unease, outrage, and the urge to take action. While many protest posters aim to inspire a feeling of identification with those depicted or to raise awareness for a particular issue, this one also serves an organizational purpose by calling on the public to take part in the mass demonstrations held to mark the tenth anniversary of the start of the First World War. The slogan "Never again!" went on to become a catchphrase that many designers would later take up in their work →146/158. Even today, a century later, it is still just as topical as ever.

From a social science point of view, protest constitutes public opposition by the less powerful against rulers and those in power – primarily against governments and economic elites. Protest is participatory "politics from below," sometimes expressed individually but usually organized collectively. Emancipatory protest posters signal the efforts by a particular social group to liberate itself from its dependence on another and to acquire social equity.

Posters have always been a central medium for visual political communication in public space. This applies to posters distributed "from above" – i.e., commissioned by governments or successful revolutionary movements[1] – as well as those "from below," which express the concerns of protesters and social movements.[2] Posters condense specific demands and messages into eye-catching, memorable graphics and texts, making them easier to grasp than complex political manifestos. Protest posters may take either a cognitive or emotional approach to the issue at hand. They summarize the facts and arguments concisely, but they may also trigger outrage, anger, or enthusiasm as a way of motivating people to advocate for the demands addressed or even to join protest movements. In research on protest and related movements, one of the central theories of mobilization is that social movements appeal to the "collective identity" of potential supporters. Visual media such as posters can play a central role, inspiring emotional identification with the subjects of the emancipation efforts. Today, analog paper protest posters are often replaced by virtual posters distributed via digital media and used to call for participation in demonstrations or petitions. Nevertheless, protest posters have not disappeared from the (material) public sphere and continue to be part of the inundation of visual messages we encounter every day on city streets.

The origins of the protest poster date back to the fifteenth century. The invention of letterpress printing with movable type made it possible for the first time to reproduce typographic printed matter by machine. In 1517, Martin Luther publicly opposed the sale of indulgences by the Catholic Church by posting his famous ninety-five theses on the door of All Saints' Church in Wittenberg for all to see. In the nineteenth century, lithographic printing made it possible to produce color posters on an industrial scale.³ Along with the invention of steam-powered paper production, this development turned posters into an affordable and popular vehicle of mass communication that could be distributed quickly in large numbers.

The political poster had its heyday in the twentieth century, when visual communication was still largely analog and had not yet moved into the digital realm as it would in the twenty-first century. The women's movement led to the founding of the Suffrage Atelier in London in 1909. This artists' collective trained women in printing techniques and encouraged them to design graphics for the political campaigns of the suffragettes, who eventually won women the right to vote in Great Britain in 1918.⁴

During the same period, successful socialist revolutionaries were drawing on the visual arts to spread their messages, and in the process they fostered avant-garde trends. Examples include Mexican muralism, which used painting and illustration to draw public attention to workers and the marginalized Indigenous population, and Russian constructivism, whose focus on photography and typography ushered in modern graphic design while establishing black, red, and white as an emblematic "left-wing" color combination. These currents would go on to shape various protest aesthetics in the twentieth century, although posters commissioned by governments can by no means be described as protests "from below."⁵

From a historical perspective, the poster proved to be an increasingly important medium of political communication in the interwar period. Even before the Nazis came to power, John Heartfield used photomontage to ridicule Adolf Hitler. One of his images, titled "Adolf the Superman Swallows Gold and Spouts Junk," was posted in large format during the Reichstag election campaign of 1932. It demonstrates that humor and satire can be employed to poke fun at rulers, creating an empowering moment for the opposition →127. Today, the disparagement of politicians and dictators is still widely used as a pictorial strategy.

The visual language portraying the heated events of May 1968 in Paris was heavily influenced by the posters produced by the Atelier Populaire. Although – or precisely because – their screen-printing technique was rudimentary and the pressure to keep up with the street fighting sometimes led to crookedly printed motifs, the many posters made at the time have etched themselves into collective visual memory →70. The group of workers depicted on one of them, with raised fists and tools in their hands, is one of the most commonly used political symbols in transnational protest imagery. With their minimalist technique and DIY aesthetic, these posters – created in the squatted printshop of the École des Beaux-Arts – authentically represent the movement behind them and its goals. Posters such as these can be reproduced quickly and inexpensively, so that mobilization via poster is not limited to affluent groups with access to high-quality equipment. And they wield their power right where the protest poster belongs – in public space, on the street, and not (only) in the protected realm of art and cultural institutions.

The year 1968 also saw the assassination of Martin Luther King, an icon of the non-violent branch of the U.S. civil rights movement. Posters bearing his portrait →163, similar to those showing Angela Davis →104, highlight how the mass distribution of images of charismatic personalities can prompt supporters to identify with a protest movement. Davis represented the more radical branch of the movement and maintained close ties with the Black Panther Party. Its "Minister of Culture," Emory Douglas, designed numerous posters marked by forceful formal language and high-impact colors, depicting Black activists – many of them armed – in self-confident poses.[6] This is a prime example of how important it is for a marginalized group to be able to represent itself in public (visual) discourse despite structural disadvantages, in imagery that goes beyond victim stereotypes.

While this rhetorical approach to portraying resistance fighters as heroes was designed to mobilize support, other protest posters sought to arouse empathy. The poster "Eat" by Tomi Ungerer, for example, is emblematic of the graphic protest against the Vietnam War and artistic solidarity between the North and South →39. It arguably achieves its haunting and disturbing effect in part by portraying "the Others" (the Vietnamese) as victims. The sight of their suffering makes viewers uncomfortable while also illustrating the risk of reproducing racist stereotypes with clichéd depictions.[7]

In the spirit of South–South solidarity, many posters produced in Cuba call on others to fight for liberation, signaling support for Vietnam, Cambodia, and Laos in their struggle against U.S. imperialism →88. In 1968, the Cuban internationalist Organization of Solidarity with the Peoples of Asia, Africa and Latin America (OSPAAAL) commissioned graphic artist Asela Maria Pérez to design a poster for the International Day of Solidarity with Latin America →65. The offset print depicts the landmass of South America as a red fist – one of the most common symbols of left-wing protest. Gripping a rifle, it sends an unmistakable message to potential invaders.[8]

Despite these examples, solidarity posters produced in the Global North are more frequently represented in European collections than those created by the affected groups from the South themselves. The graphic design collective Fireworks, active in Los Angeles and San Francisco, expressed its solidarity with Chilean resistance against Augusto Pinochet in a 1983 poster with the text: "Down with the Chilean Dictatorship! Support the Popular Resistance!" →22. Designed in the style of the Atelier Populaire, the screen print in the typical socialist colors of red, black, and white depicts an archaic street battle as viewed from the perspective of the Chilean resistance fight-ers standing firm against the dictator's tanks.

In the late 1970s and early 1980s, the women's movement advocated for its cause with a very different poster rhetoric. The Guerrilla Girls denounced sexism in the art world and society by presenting the facts with a heavy dose of irony, attempting to enlighten the public in a humorous way →18. Another strategy is to depict pain and physical suffering, which in principle anyone can empathize with, regardless of their political views. The facial expressions of the woman in Jeannie Friedman's "Women Unite!" →16 and in the poster produced by the graphics collective Fireworks →20 can be interpreted as conveying militant anger or even pain. In the latter poster, blood dripping from a wire coat hanger viscerally conveys the physical pain of women forced by an abortion ban to resort to make-shift, non-medical procedures. In Turkey, posters produced for the campaign "Our Bodies Belong to Us – No to Sexual Abuse!" likewise depict women's physical and mental pain, here with a focus on the rights of sex workers →15.

The role that posters play in international political campaigns is demonstrated by commissioned works for large non-governmental organizations such as Amnesty International →95.[9] The campaign material is usually available online for download and use in local street protests. Conversely, move-ments that are less strategically organized but instead develop organically on the Web in a decentralized manner often enlist the assistance of graphic designers to create posters proclaiming their goals. They include the #MeToo movement, which emerged in 2017. Its enormous reach was illustrated typo-graphically by graphic artist Lahav Halevy, among others →133. A similarly widespread impact generated by purely typographical means was achieved by a poster for the women's protests in Iran, which were triggered by the violent death of Jina Mahsa Amini in 2022. The studio of the exiled Iranian designer Golnar Kat Rahmani, who today lives in Berlin, chose a dynamic rendering of the slogan "Zan, Zendegi, Āzādi" (Woman, Life, Liberty) as a way of addressing the Iranian diaspora in their native Persian →137.

During the Arab Spring in the 2010s, protest movements in the Middle East mainly used digital channels and images on social media to coordinate and mobilize. Posters from the civil society uprising in Syria, such as those produced by the anonymous collective Alshaab Alsori Aref Tarekh (The Syrian People Know Their Way), were distributed exclusively online. They show that posters can still mobilize street protests even when it is too dangerous to display these posters on the street itself.[10] In this case, terms such as "social media wall" demonstrate that digital images are still attached to a "wall" even in the digital space.

Protest graphics used by social movements from the 2000s onwards cover a broad spectrum of themes – from flight and migration →55/139 to climate change →73 and the recognition of women of color as pioneers of emancipa-tion →91/121. In 2020, as part of the Celebrate People's History series by the Justseeds Artists' Cooperative, Brazilian designer Camila Rosa created a post-er →125 that illustrates the various factors contributing to the transnational impact of the emancipatory protest poster. Her poster provides information on social and political resistance movements such as the Movimento dos Trabalhadores Sem Terra (MST), one of the largest social movements in Latin America. At the same time, it features images of aesthetically rendered yet combative identification figures designed to empower others. The poster appeals both on a cognitive level – through logical arguments – and on an emotional level – through the women depicted. Some of them have angry faces and one is raising her fist. Just like protest itself, emancipatory de-sign can reinforce a sense of collective identity, of belonging to a community. Protest posters are capable of strengthening the cohesion of a movement both internally and externally by making social groups and their demands visible in public space and thus in public discourse – as effectively today as a century ago.

51

1   David King, *Russian Revolutionary Posters: From Civil War to Socialist Realism, from Bolshevism to the End of Stalinism*, London 2015.
2   Lisa Bogerts, *The Aesthetics of Rule and Resistance: Analyzing Political Street Art in Latin America*, New York 2022.
3   Bettina Richter, "From Pasquino to Anonymous," in Basil Rogger, Jonas Voegeli, Ruedi Widmer, and Museum für Gestaltung Zürich (eds.), *Protest: The Aesthetics of Resistance*, Zurich 2018, pp. 378–380.
4   Liz McQuiston, *Protest! A History of Social and Political Protest Graphics,* London 2019, pp. 42–49; Gerda Breuer, "Suffragettes: Early Corporate and Communication Design in England," in Breuer, *HerStories in Graphic Design: Dialogue, Continuity, Self-Empowerment; Women Graphic Designers from 1880 until Today*, Berlin 2023, pp. 102–113.
5   Bogerts, 2022.
6   https://collections.library.yale.edu/catalog/33215778.
7   McQuiston, 2019, p. 100.
8   Richard Frick, *Das trikontinentale Solidaritätsplakat*, Bern 2003.
9   Amnesty International, Joanne Rippon, *The Art of Protest: A Visual History of Dissent and Resistance*, Woodbridge 2019.
10 www.britishmuseum.org/collection/term/BIOG246525.

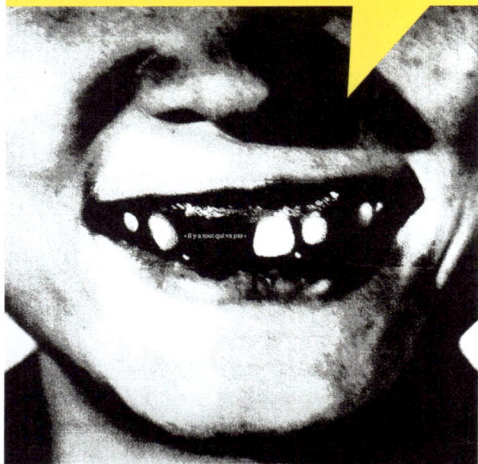

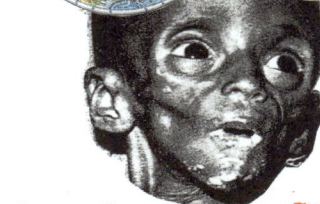

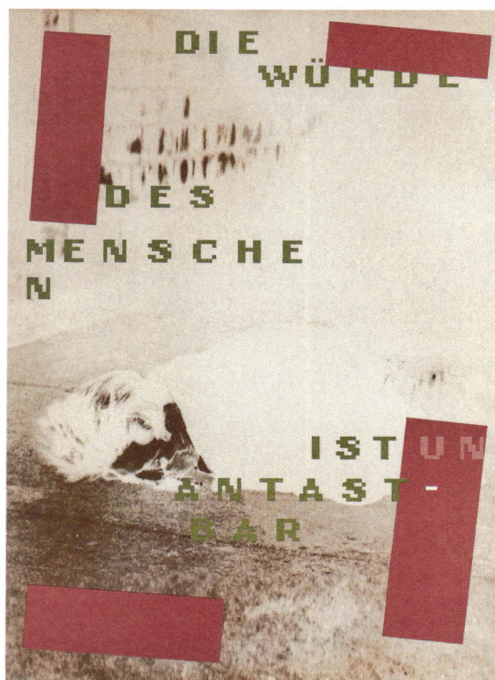

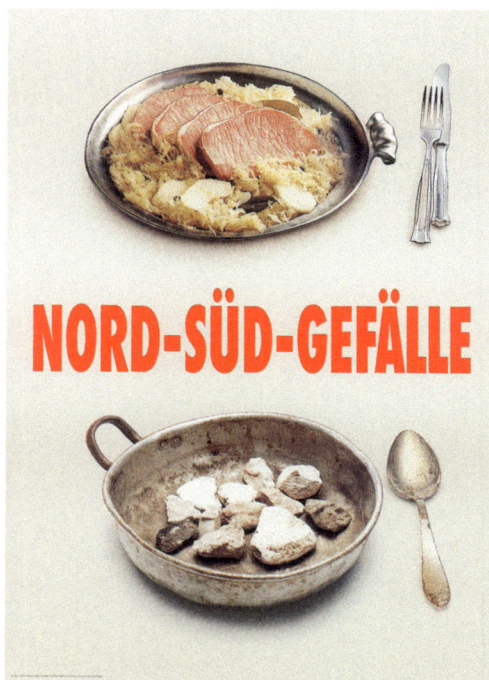

56 Gérard Paris-Clavel
    Pas d'achat, pas de bonheur
    2002

57 Agil / Sascha Lobe
    Die Würde des Menschen ist unantastbar
    1993

58 Gérard Paris-Clavel
    Money World
    1992

59 Klaus Staeck
    Nord-Süd-Gefälle
    1991

ART DIRECTOR/DESIGNER SIGEL SHIMO'OKA   PHOTOGRAPHER SEIJI YAMADA

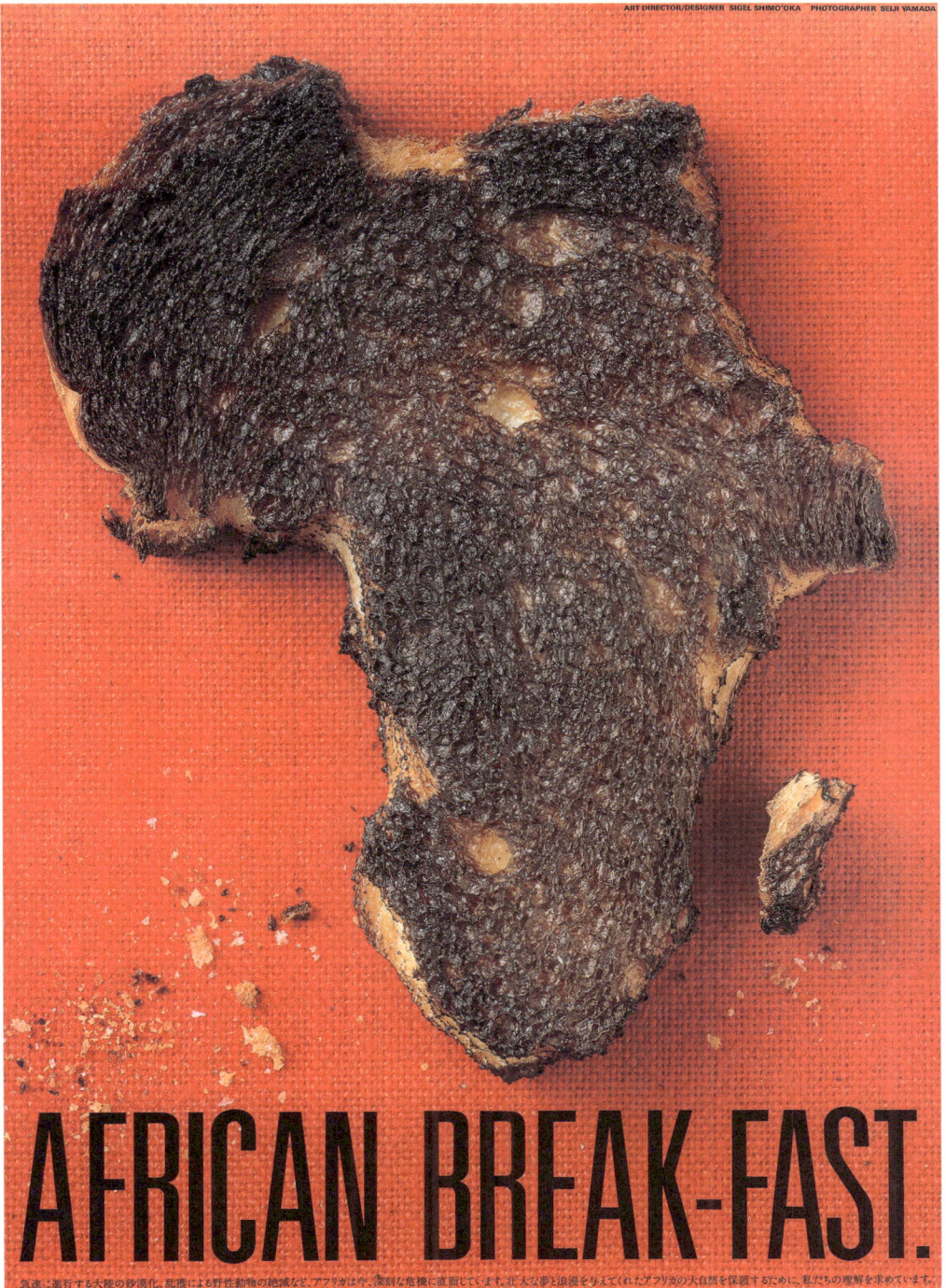

AFRICAN BREAK-FAST.

急速に進行する大陸の砂漠化、乱獲による野性動物の絶滅など、アフリカは今、深刻な危機に直面しています。壮大な夢と浪漫を与えてくれたアフリカの大自然を保護するために、私たちの理解を求めています。

60   Sigel Shimo'Oka
       African Break-Fast.
       1997

FREE SOUTH AFRICA

61   Keith Haring
     Free South Africa
     1985

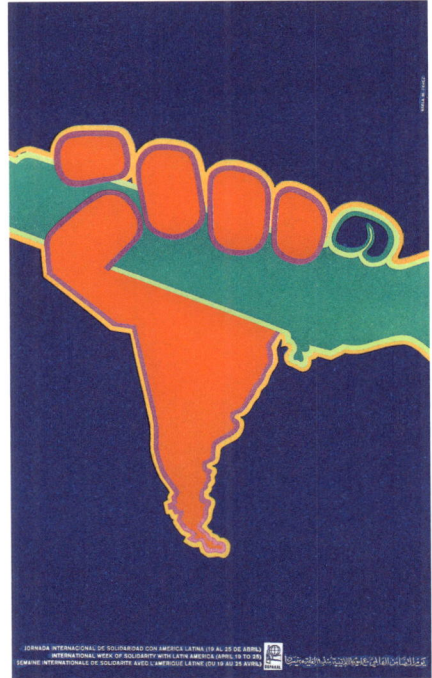

62   Anonym
        ¡Cese!
        1986

63   Reto Coaz
        Modell Davos.05
        2004

64   Ulrike Würfel
        Afrika / Afrika / Afrika (…)
        2016

65   Asela Maria Pérez
        Jornada internacional de solidaridad
        con America Latina
        1968

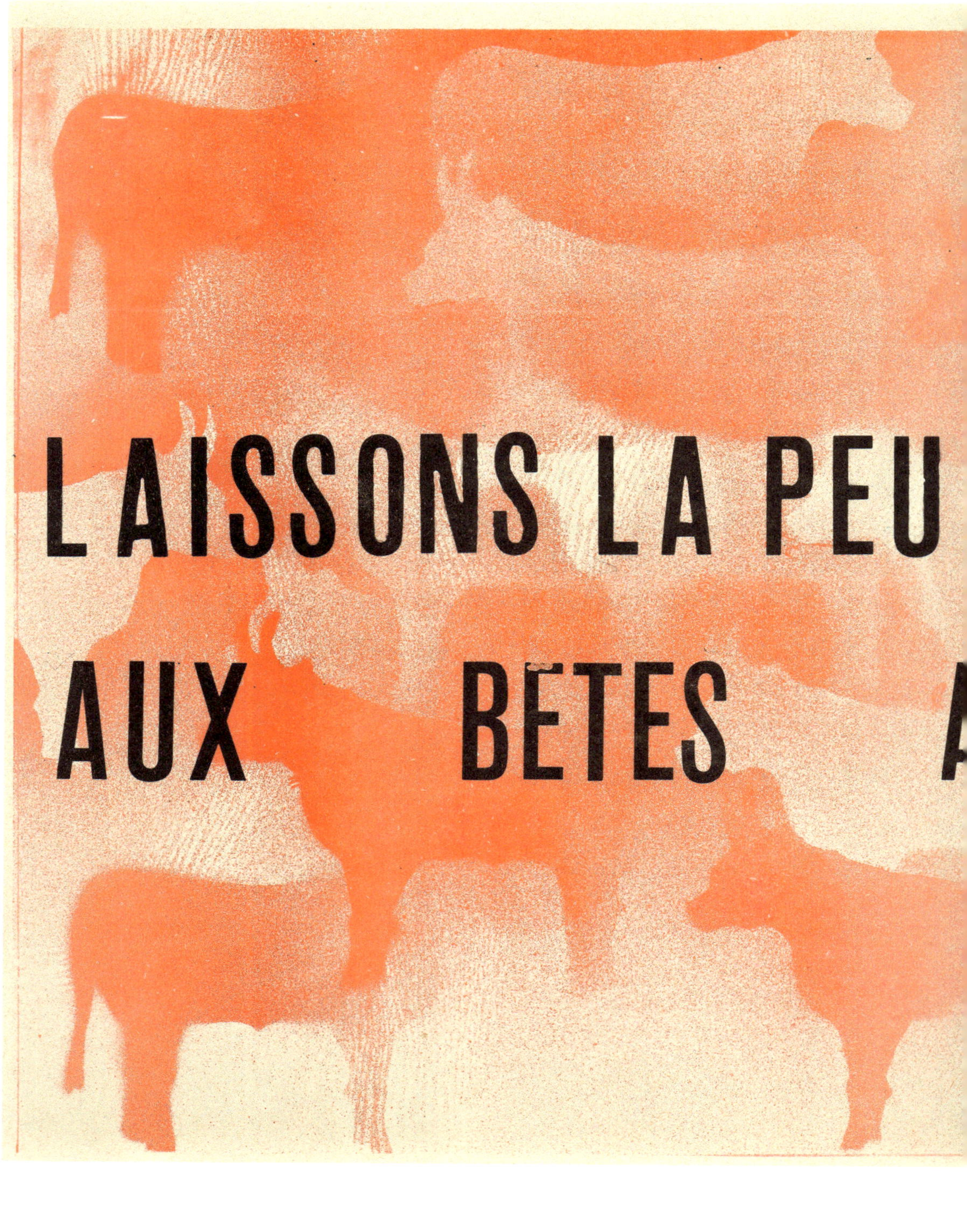

66 Atelier Populaire
Laissons la peur du rouge
aux bêtes à cornes
1968

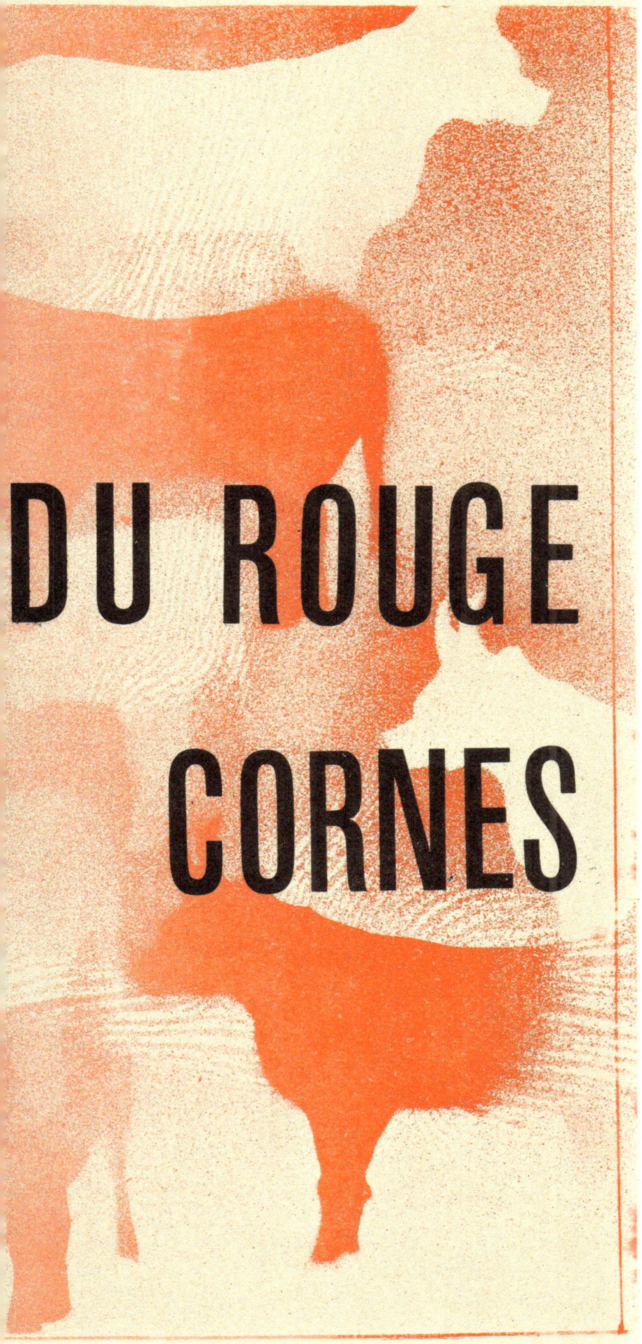
DU ROUGE
CORNES

COEXISTENCE

67   Grapus
      Picasso 28.12.1961 / Grapus 28.12.1987
      1987

68   Piotr Młodozeniec
      Coexist / Coexistence
      2000

Solidarische Formen: Zeichen und Symbole

Silas Munro

Protestplakate sind voller Zeichen und Symbole. Das ist keine Überraschung, bildet die visuelle Abstraktion schliesslich das Fundament des Grafikdesigns. Doch sind Protestsymbole schwieriger zu gestalten als die meisten anderen Designaufträge. Sie müssen im Moment einer Protestbewegung rasch entworfen werden, sind oftmals nur aus der Ferne und üblicherweise in Bewegung zu sehen, hochgehalten von Demonstrierenden. Häufig transportieren sie komplexe geopolitische Themen und wollen gleichzeitig die Emotionen ansprechen. Shigeo Fukudas Plakat «Victory 1945», das 1975 gedruckt und veröffentlicht wurde, hat eine eindringliche Botschaft: Zu sehen ist eine mit dickem schwarzen Strich gezeichnete Schiffskanone auf leuchtend gelbem Hintergrund, deren überdimensionale Kugel gegen sich selbst gerichtet ist →78. Ein einziges, stark vereinfachtes Bild bringt die Kritik an Japans problematischer Rolle im Zweiten Weltkrieg auf den Punkt.

Designerinnen und Designer von Protestgrafiken verwenden häufig semiotische Formeln und nehmen dabei Bezug auf bereits erfolgreiche visuelle Strategien und kompositorische Zugänge. Tauben stehen als gängiges Symbol für Frieden, Totenköpfe für den Tod, Hakenkreuze für Nazis, Waffen und Bomben für Krieg, erhobene Fäuste für Aufstände. Andere wiederkehrende Motive sind der afrikanische Kontinent, religiöse Symbole oder Zielscheiben. Es ist eine Art grafische Solidarität, die sowohl ästhetisch als auch politisch motiviert ist. Jeannie Friedmans «Women Unite!» →16 aus dem Jahr 1976 liegt eine posterisierte Schwarz-Weiss-Fotografie zugrunde, die dem Plakat «So Long as Women Are not Free the People Are not Free» des See Red Women's Workshop aus dem Jahr 1978 ähnelt →21. «Libérez Angela Davis», das von einer Vereinigung kommunistischer Studierender in Frankreich entworfen wurde, setzt für Davis' ikonisches Afro-Look-Porträt eine posterisierte Vorlage zeichnerisch um →104. Diese Plakate greifen die avantgardistische Fotomontage des 20. Jahrhunderts auf, hervorgegangen aus Experimenten mit kontrastreichen Belichtungen und Fotogrammen in der Dunkelkammer, bei denen ohne Kamera symbolische Bilder entstanden – kontrastreiche Techniken, die sich durch die Ausbildung und Veröffentlichungen an renommierten europäischen Designschulen, viele davon mit Sitz in der Schweiz, etablierten.

69   Atelier Populaire
     Non
     1968

70   Atelier Populaire
     La lutte continue
     1968

Solidarity in Forms: Signs and Symbols

Protest posters are full of signs and symbols. This is not a surprise, as visual abstraction is the bread and butter of graphic design, but protest signs have it harder than most design briefs. They must be created quickly in the moment of a movement, and they are often seen from a distance, usually in motion, in the hands of a marching protester. They frequently convey complex geopolitical issues while simultaneously making an emotional appeal. Shigeo Fukuda's poster "Victory 1945," printed and posted in 1975, makes a strong point by showing a bold black drawing of a battleship's cannon with its oversized bullet pointing back at itself on a bright yellow color field →78. In one reduced image, you see an absurd critique of the problematic legacy of Japan's role in the Second World War.

One way designers of protest graphics do their job is through semiotic short-hand – referencing the successful visual strategies and compositional approaches of other designers. Common symbols include doves for peace, skulls for death, swastikas for Nazis, guns and bombs for war, and raised fists for uprisings. Other recurring motifs include the African continent, religious symbols, and targets. This is a form of graphic solidarity that is both aesthetically and politically driven. Jeannie Friedman's 1976 "Women Unite" →16 uses a posterized black-and-white photograph that looks like the 1978 poster "So Long as Women Are Not Free the People Are Not Free" by See Red Women's Workshop →21. "Libérez Angela Davis," designed by a union of communist students in France, used a poster as a template for a drawn version of Davis's iconic Afro-styled portrait →104. These posters tap into the histories of twentieth-century avant-garde montage, emerging from darkroom experiments in high-contrast exposures and photograms that produced symbolic images without a camera. These high-contrast techniques were canonized by the pedagogy and publishing activities of noted European design schools, many based in Switzerland.

Is your baby safe?
Save your child from the polluted water.

71   Stefano Rovai
      31:1:2000
      2000

72   Atelier Bagarre / Hakim Abel Ben Youcef
      Paris / 2024 / Control
      2024

73   Naoki Hirai
      Is Your Baby Safe?
      2001

74   Anonym
      Am 26. April 1986 explodierte im Atomkraftwerk
      von Tschernobyl ein Reaktorblock.
      2011

Piär Amrein
Terracotta
2019

Klaus Staeck
Coca-Cola präsentiert
1994

VICTORY 1945

77   Marlena Buczek Smith
      [ohne Text – no text]
      2009

78   Shigeo Fukuda
      Victory 1945
      1975

79   Savaş Çekiç
      [ohne Text – no text]
      1998

80   Tomaso Marcolla
      [ohne Text – no text]
      2015

81   Lex Drewinski
      Racism
      1993

82   Chaz Maviyane-Davies   83   Victore Design Works / James Victore
      Globalisation   Celebrate Columbus 1492–1992
      2005   1992

84 Lahav Halevy
Syrian Killer
2016

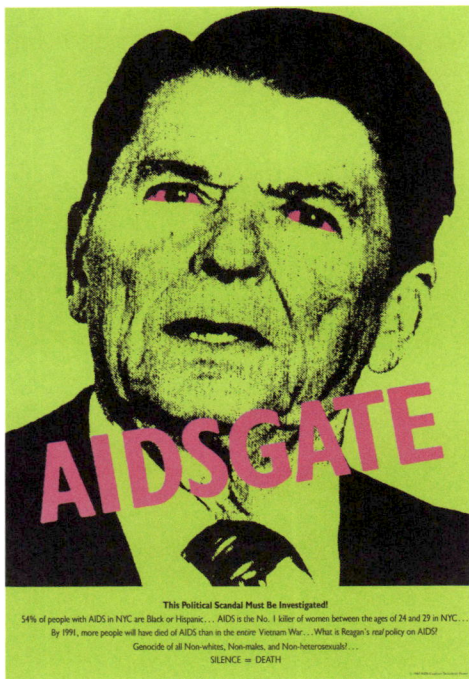

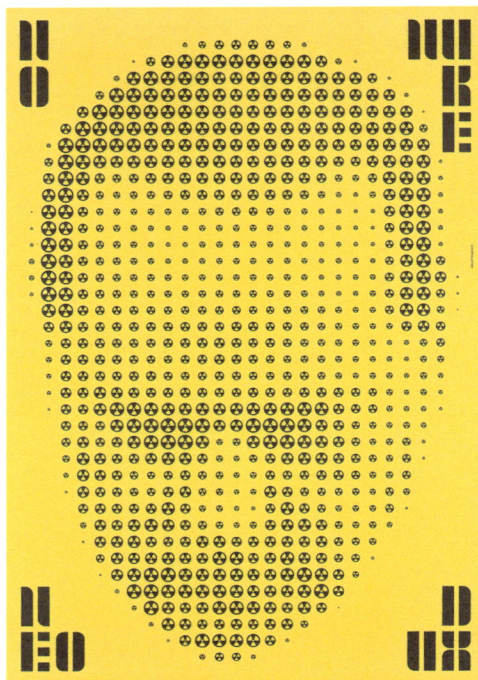

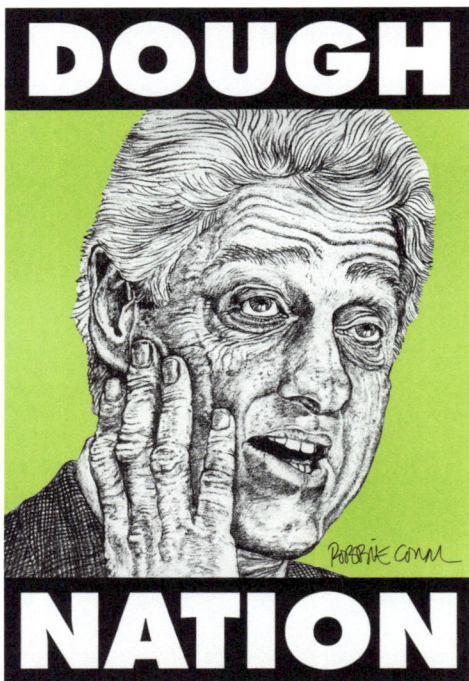

85   Gran Fury
      Aidsgate
      1987

86   Robbie Conal
      Dough Nation
      1997

87   Mauro Bubbico
      No Nuke / No Neo Dux
      2011

88   Luis Balaguer
      Jornada continental de apoyo a Vietnam,
      Cambodia y Laos
      1969

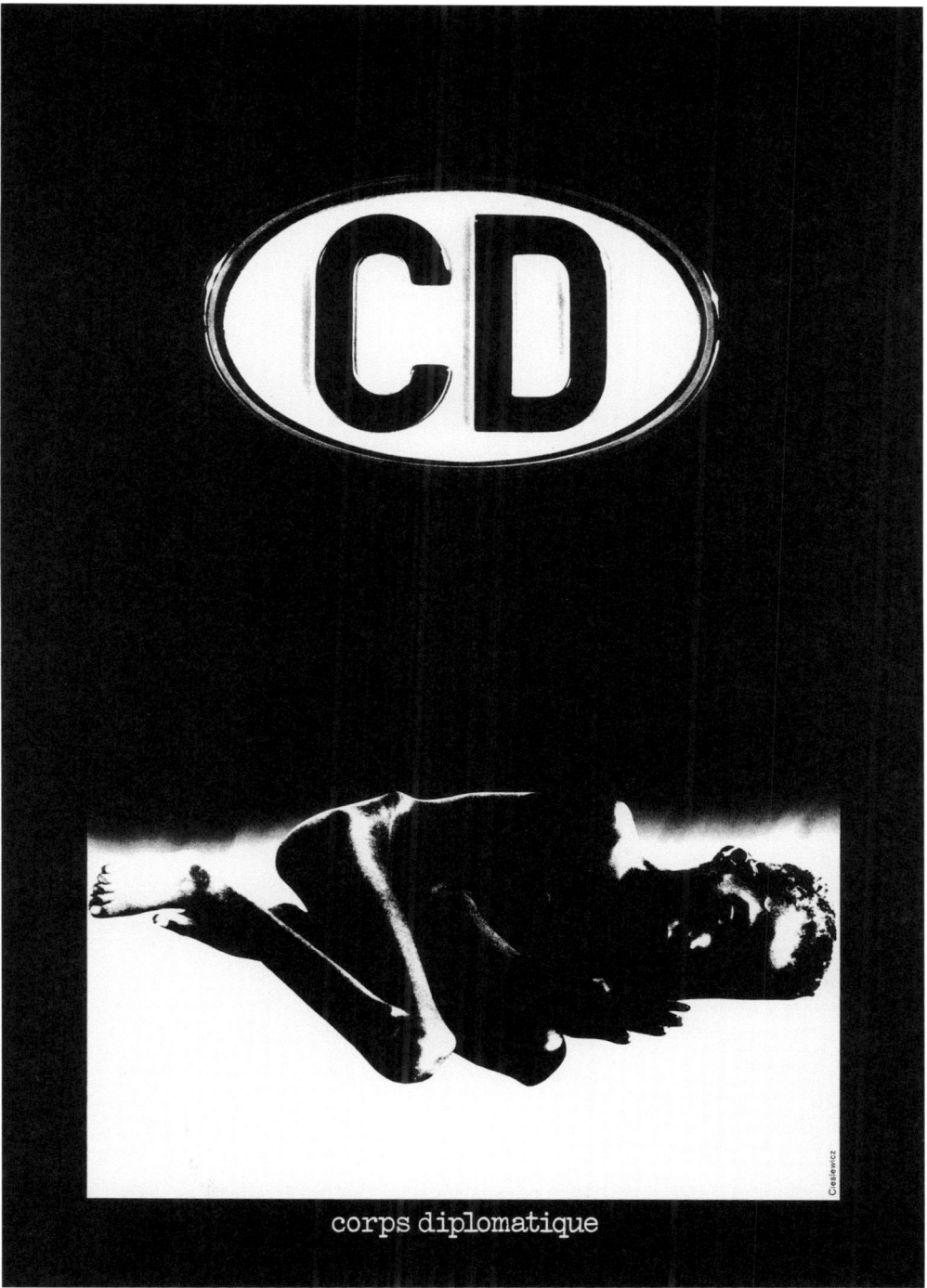

89 Roman Cieślewicz
CD / Corps diplomatique
1994

The poster reads:

¡El Agua es nuestra carajo!

Celebrate People's History

The water is ours damnit! under pressure from the World-Bolivian government, sold off system of it's 3rd largest city behind closed doors, to multi investors including the Bechtel over night people were asked to pay 25% of their income for water including collected rainfall and backyard wells. Months of protest ensued. The country was declared under martial law but thousands took to the streets. This combined with international activist pressure forced Bechtel to flee the country. Despite subse--quent attempts to sue Bolivia for $25M in loss of "potential profit", the people of Coch--abamba succeeded in defeating a corporate giant and regaining control of one of life's most necessary resources.

In 1999, Bank, the the water Cochabamba -national corporation.

art by Swoon, more posters: www.justseeds.org, printed by Stumptown Printers, April 2005

90   Swoon
      ¡El Agua es nuestra carajo!
      2005

So journer Truth, born Isabella (Belle) Baumfree, c.1797 - November 26, 1883, was an African-American abolitionist and women's rights activist. Truth was born into slavery in Swartekill, NY but escaped with her infant daughter to freedom in 1826. After going to court to recover her son in 1828 she became the 1st black woman to win such a case against a white man. She gave herself the name SOJOURNER TRUTH in 1843 after she became convinced that God had called her to leave the city and go into the countryside "testifying to the hope that was in her." Her best known speech was delivered extemporaneously in 1851 at the Ohio Women's Rights Convention in Akron, OH. The speech became widely known during the civil war by the title "Ain't I a Woman?" Well?

$10. REWARD —Absconded from the subscriber's dwelling, on the 6th instant, the negro girl BELLE, aged about 30; speaks English and Dutch; has lost her front teeth; very dark skin: took with her her daughter, a mulatto, aged about 7. She has a daughter on Girod street, No 185, and may go there at night. She absented herself without cause.

CELEBRATE PEOPLE'S HISTORY

91   Chip Thomas
Sojourner Truth, born Isabella (Belle) Baumfree
2021

92 Asamblea de Artistas Revolucionarios
de Oaxaca (ASARO)
Muerte al capitalismo
2007

Kunst, Widerstand und Erinnerung: Grafik als Mittel der politischen Kommunikation

Die Asamblea de Artistas Revolucionarios de Oaxaca (ASARO) entstand am 29. Oktober 2006 im Zuge eines Streiks von Lehrkräften in Oaxaca, dem eine massive gesellschaftliche Mobilisierung und die gewaltsame Reaktion der Staatsregierung folgten. Die Gründung von ASARO war eine unmittelbare und symbolische Antwort darauf. Während die Regierung versuchte, die Spuren der Volksproteste auszulöschen, übernahmen wir, eine Gruppe von Künstlerinnen und Künstlern, die Strasse und hinterliessen unsere grafischen Botschaften an den Wänden – Botschaften der Verurteilung, des Widerstands und der Solidarität mit dem Volk von Oaxaca. Bei uns gab es keine Hierarchien, und wir wählten die Anonymität, um unsere Identität zu bewahren und uns dem Egokult und der künstlerischen Anerkennung zu verweigern.

Gezielt setzten wir Gravuren, Schablonen und andere grafische Techniken der Urban Art ein, die den Vorteil haben, dass sie kostengünstig und einfach zu reproduzieren sind und sich den urbanen Raum wirksam aneignen können. So konnten wir eine zugängliche Bildsprache entwickeln, die es geschafft hat, sich im kollektiven Gedächtnis und in der historischen Erzählung von Oaxaca zu verankern. Unsere Arbeit ist von lokalen Symbolen wie Maiskolben, den Gesichtern indigener Menschen, Schlangen und revolutionären Persönlichkeiten geprägt, die nicht nur eine kulturelle Identität beschwören, sondern ihre politische Bedeutung auch in die Gegenwart transportieren. Was als lokale Reaktion begann, wurde zu einer Bewegung mit globaler Resonanz. Mit unseren Grafiken haben wir die Krise um das Verschwinden von Frauen in Nordmexiko, die Wasserknappheit in verschiedenen Regionen, das Verschwinden von Studierenden und andere soziale Konflikte, die zahlreiche Gemeinschaften weltweit betreffen, sichtbar gemacht.

Die Kunst von ASARO spiegelt Unterdrückung und soziale Kämpfe nicht passiv wider, sondern interpretiert diese, verleiht ihnen eine neue Bedeutung und präsentiert sie vor einem ethischen und ästhetischen Horizont. Unsere Arbeiten beschränken sich nicht darauf, gesellschaftliche Missstände anzuprangern, sondern sie dokumentieren, archivieren und übermitteln Geschichten aus der Perspektive des Volkes.

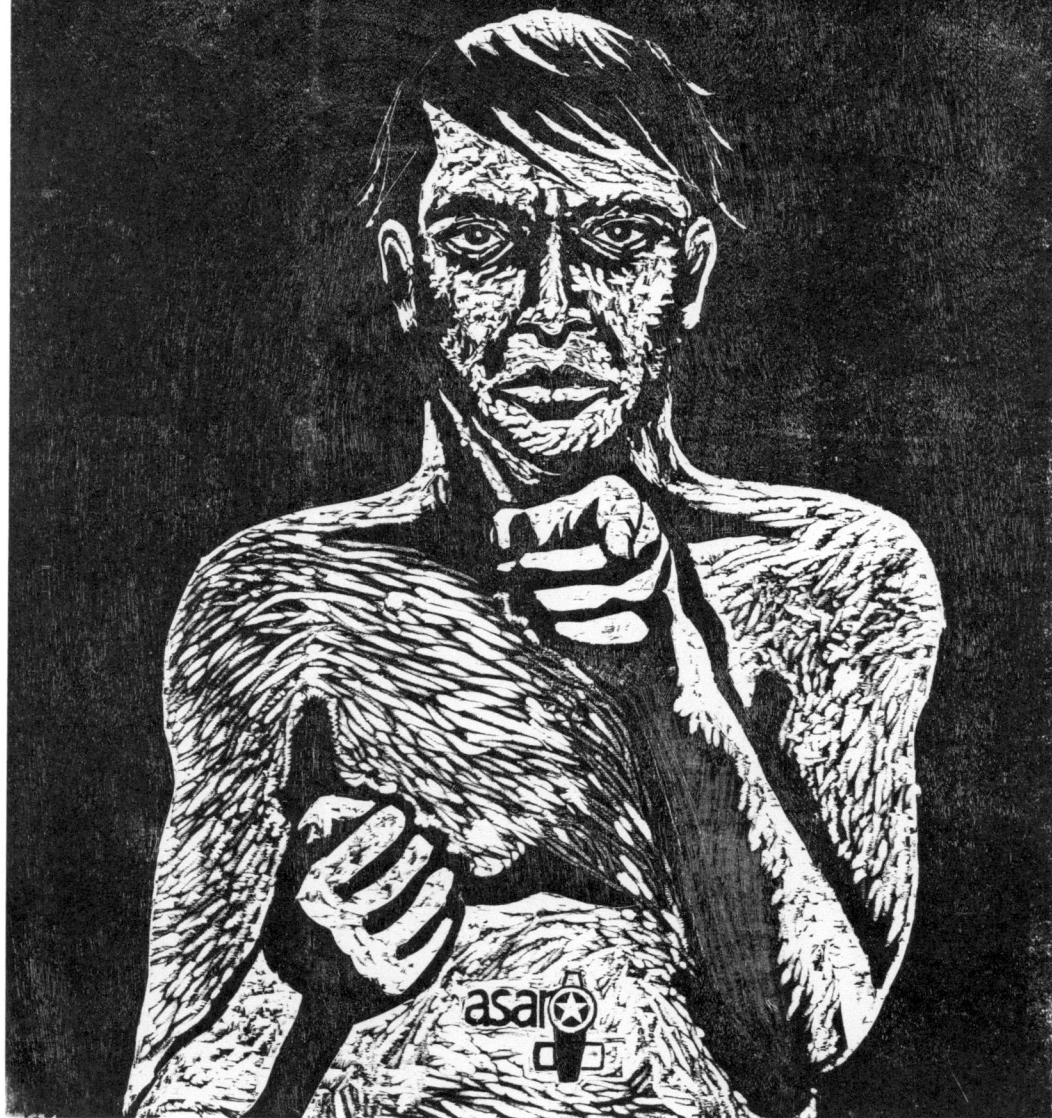

93   Asamblea de Artistas Revolucionarios
      de Oaxaca (ASARO)
      ¡Pueblo! ¡Defiende tu petróleo!
      2007

Art, Resistance, and Memory: Graphics as a Means of Political Communication

ASARO

Asamblea de Artistas Revolucionarios de Oaxaca (ASARO) emerged on October 29, 2006, in the context of a teachers' strike in Oaxaca that resulted in a massive social mobilization and a violent reaction from the state government. The creation of ASARO was an immediate and symbolic response: while the government tried to erase the traces of the popular protest, we, as a group of artists, took to the streets to leave our graphic mark on walls with messages of condemnation, resistance, and solidarity with the Oaxacan people. ASARO was structured horizontally, and we chose anonymity to preserve our identities and to reject the cult of ego and artistic recognition.

Through the strategic use of engraving, stencils, and other urban graphic techniques – which benefit from low cost, ease of reproduction, and effectiveness in the occupation of urban space – we have articulated an accessible visual language that has managed to anchor its discourse in the collective memory and the historical narrative of Oaxaca. Our work is nourished by local symbols such as corncobs, Indigenous faces, snakes, and revolutionary figures, which not only evoke a cultural identity, but also project their political meaning into the present. What began as a local response became a movement with a global echo. Through its graphics, ASARO has made visible the crisis surrounding the disappearance of women in northern Mexico, water shortages in various regions, the disappearance of students, and other social conflicts that affect various communities worldwide.

ASARO's art does not passively reflect repression or social struggle, but interprets, re-signifies, and projects it as an ethical and aesthetic horizon. Our works are not limited to denouncing social ills; they also document, archive, and transmit stories from a popular perspective.

Got oil?

94   Nenad Cizl
      Got Oil?
      2004

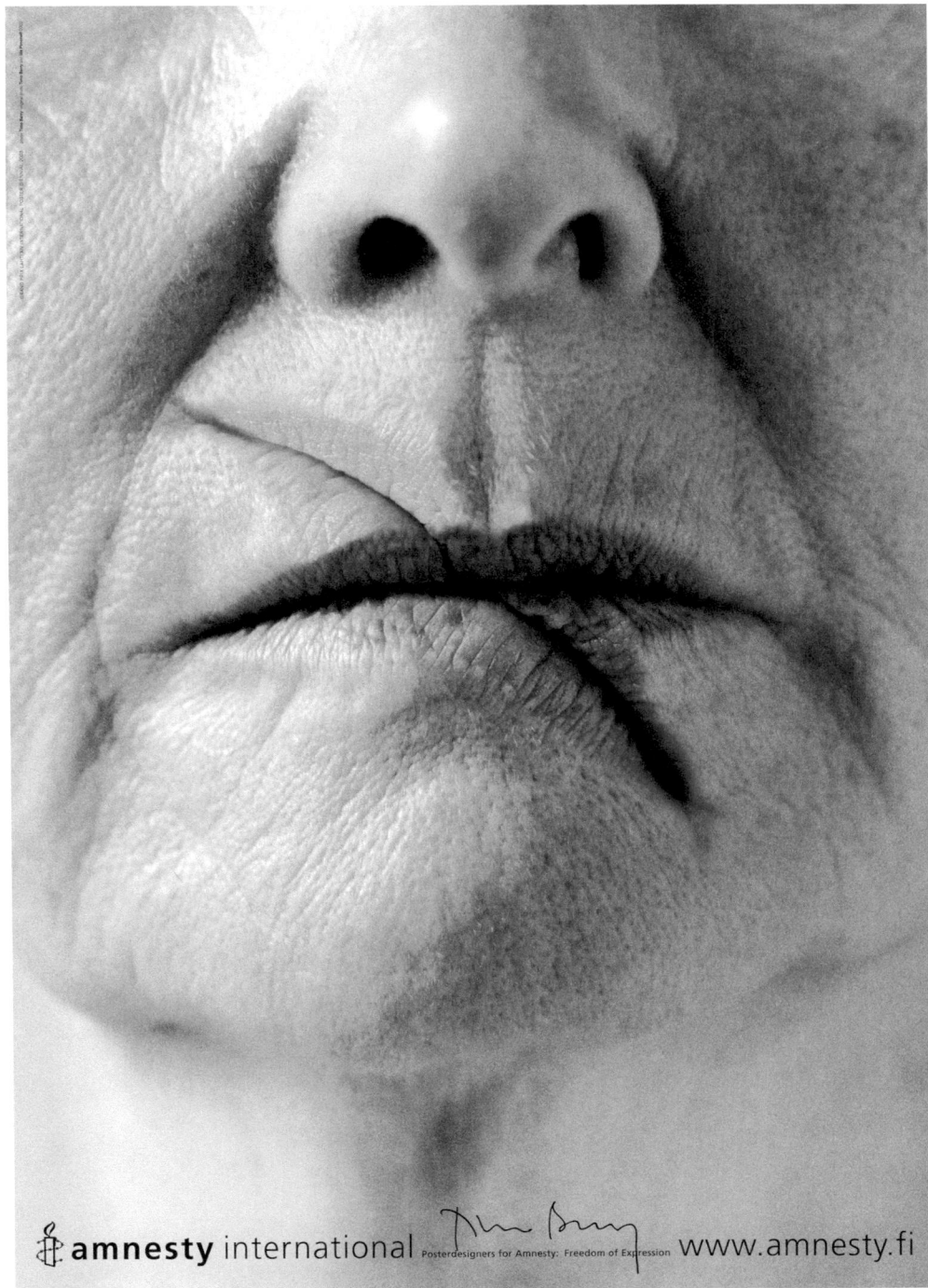

95　Suunnittelutoimisto Both / Timo Berry
Amnesty International / Recht auf
freie Meinungsäusserung
2003

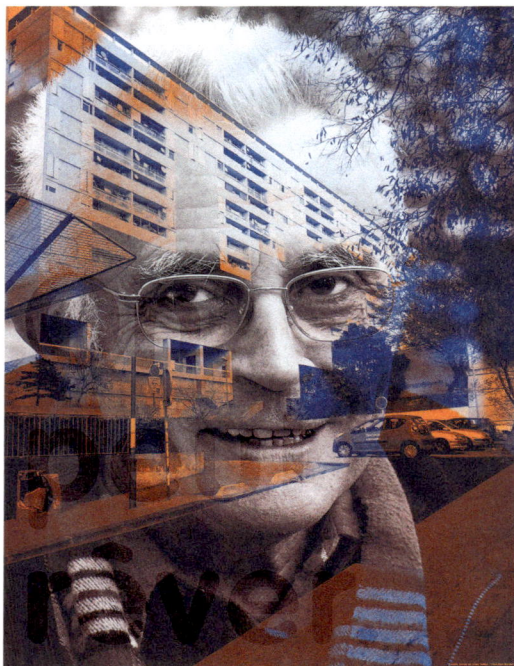

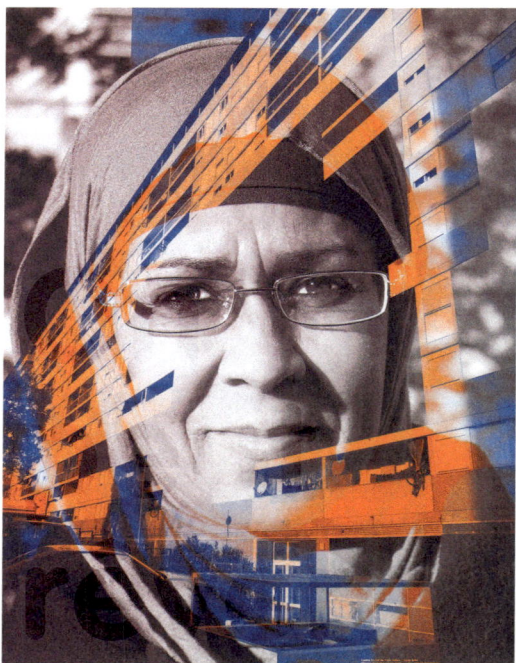

96–   Vincent Perrottet   99   Vincent Perrottet
98   On peut rêver.   Et le respect ??
       2011   2011

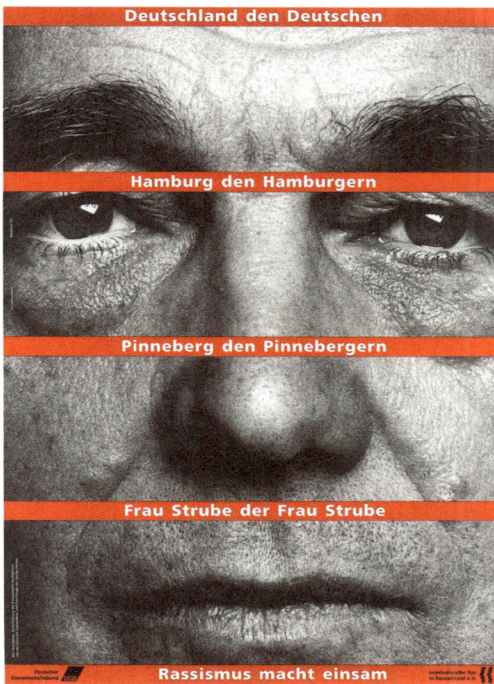

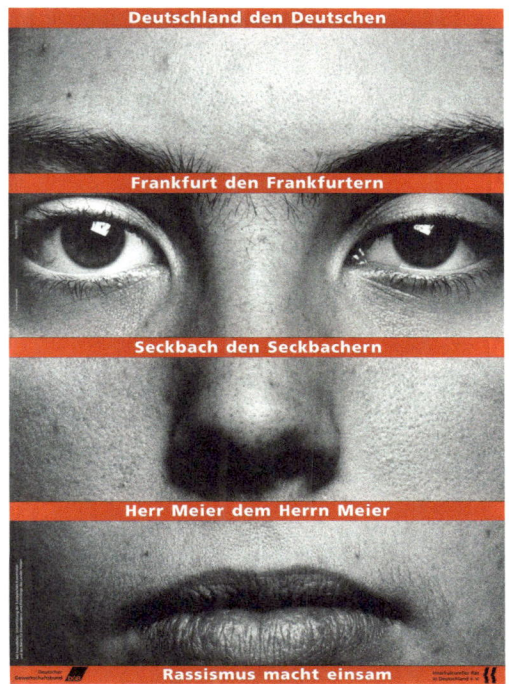

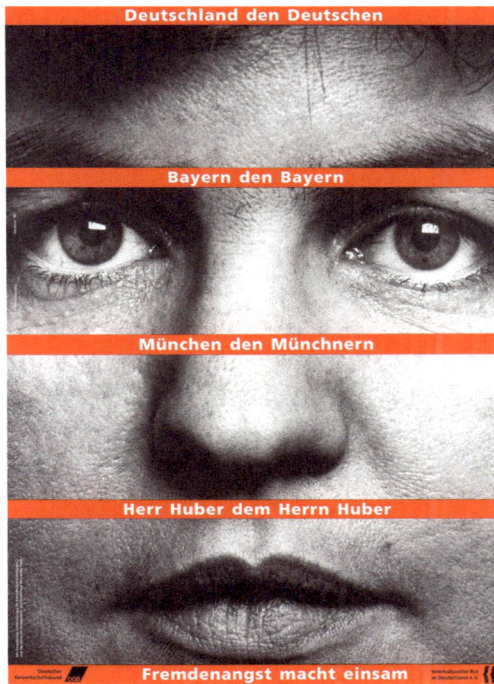

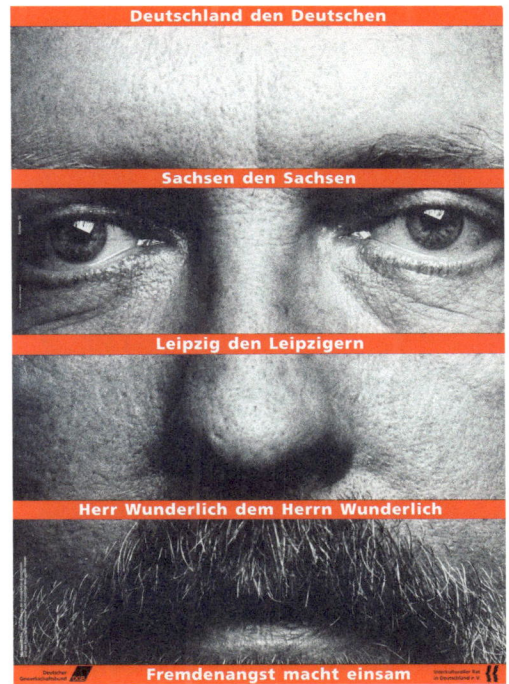

100– Gunter Rambow
103 Deutschland den Deutschen
     1995

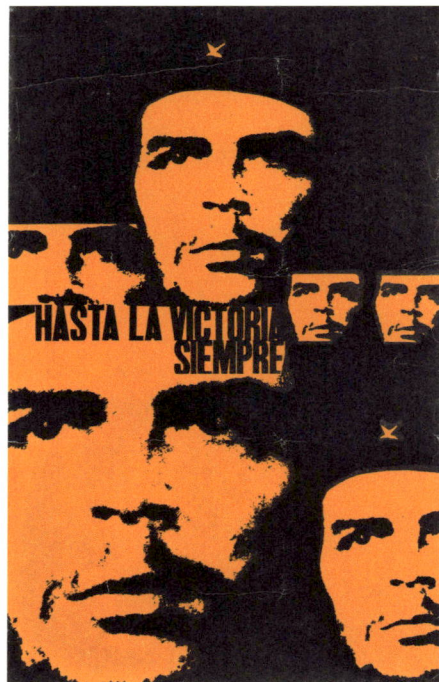

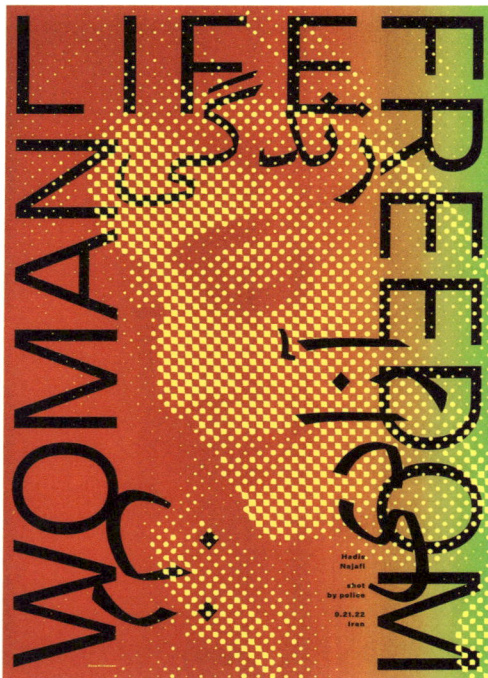

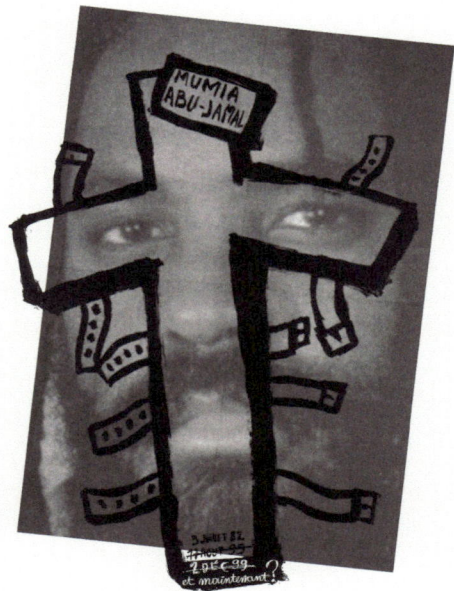

104   Anonym
        Libérez Angela Davis
        ca. 1970

105   Fons Hickmann m23 / Fons Hickmann
        Woman Life Freedom
        2023

106   Ñiko
        Hasta la victoria siempre
        1968

107   Jean-Claude Blanchard
        Mumia Abu-Jamal
        1999

Idol und Feindbild

Bettina Richter

Nicht nur das Wahlplakat bedient sich weltweit der Personalisierung:
Auch für das Widerstandsplakat erweist sich diese Strategie als besonders
geeignet, um als Blickfänger zu funktionieren und schnellen Konsens
zu erzielen. Sowohl für Vor- als auch für Feindbilder bieten sich im globalen
Kontext Figuren an, die bereits internationale Aufmerksamkeit erzielt
haben. So lieferte Alberto Kordas berühmte Fotografie von Ernesto «Che»
Guevara die Vorlage für sein millionenfach reproduziertes Porträt →106.
Als kollektiv adoptierte Leitfigur können Idole zum beliebig einsetzbaren
Symbol erstarren und von der Konsum- und Popkultur vereinnahmt werden.
Eine Wiederbelebung, die die biografische Anbindung sucht, kann dem
entgegenwirken. Beispiele dafür sind Plakate, die Mumia Abu-Jamal →107
oder Martin Luther King →108/163 würdigen. Beide stehen in Geschichte
und Gegenwart noch immer dezidiert für ihren Kampf gegen Rassismus
und Apartheid.

Häufiger äussert sich grafischer Protest in der Demontage der politischen
Elite und des durch sie verkörperten Systems. Zynisch, ironisch oder
humorvoll inszeniert, werden autoritäre Führerfiguren auf ein menschliches
Mass zurechtgestutzt. Die Dekonstruktion der Mächtigen antwortet
dabei immer auf eine vorausgehende mediale Konstruktion ihres Images.
Einerseits vermögen plakatfremde, künstlerische Gestaltungsverfahren
Aufmerksamkeit zu erregen, die sich gezielt von der Werbeästhetik absetzen.
Andererseits kann gerade das bewusste Spiel mit der Rhetorik der Massen-
kommunikation deren Wirkungsweisen unterlaufen. John Heartfields
aufklärerische Fotomontagen von Adolf Hitler →127 sind in ein internationales
Protestrepertoire eingegangen, was Bildzitate belegen →3. Ganz anders
argumentieren die Plakate des Atelier Populaire vom Pariser Mai 1968, die
auf lapidare, witzige und lustvolle Weise das Bild des französischen
Präsidenten konterkarieren →30.

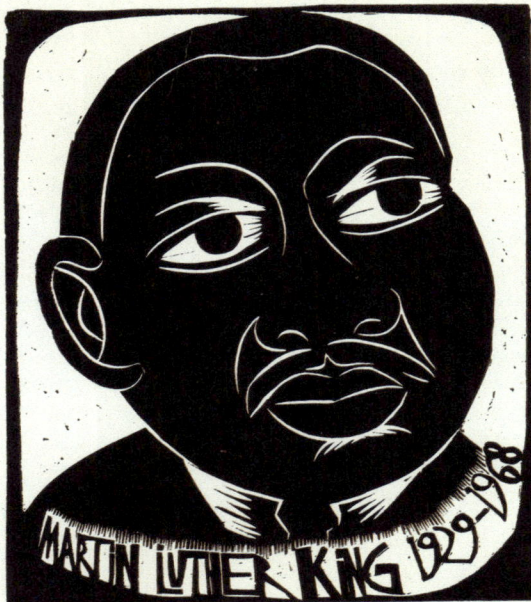

108   Paul Peter Piech
      I Have a Dream
      1983

Election posters are not the only works that use personalization to attract attention worldwide. This strategy has also proven effective in resistance posters, transforming them into eye-catching works capable of achieving a quick consensus. In the global context, figures already in the international limelight can serve as either role models or images of the enemy. Alberto Korda's famous photograph of Ernesto "Che" Guevara provided the template for a portrait →106 that has been reproduced millions of times in posters. As collectively adopted leaders, idols may become frozen symbols used for arbitrary purposes or appropriated by consumer and pop culture. A revival that seeks a true biographical connection can counteract this tendency. Examples include the posters honoring Mumia Abu-Jamal →107 and Martin Luther King →108/163, both of whom stand for the resolute fight against racism and apartheid, past and present.

More frequently, graphic forms of protest are used to dismantle the political elite and the system they embody. Portrayed cynically, ironically, or comically, authoritarian leaders are cut down to human size, their deconstruction always responding to an image already developed and propagated by the media. Artistic design methods not usually found in posters may cause a stir by deliberately diverging from advertising aesthetics. At the same time, the deliberate toying with the rhetoric of mass communication can undermine the way such communication works. John Heartfield's revealing photomontages of Adolf Hitler →127 have become part of an international protest repertoire, as illustrated by a range of visual quotations →3. By contrast, the posters produced by the Atelier Populaire during the Paris protests of May 1968 take a very different approach, evidently delighting in countering the usual image of the French president in succinct and witty fashion →30.

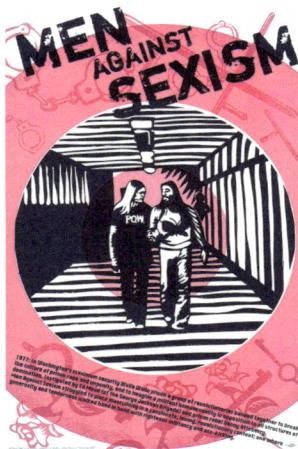

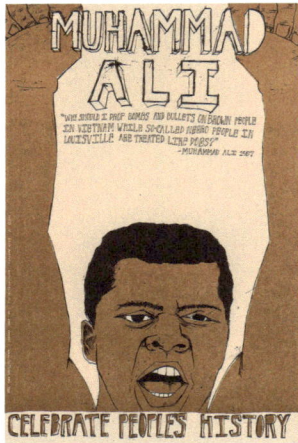

109 John Jennings
James Baldwin
2015

110 Brett Colley
"I cannot stand and sing
the anthem. (…)"
2020

111 Lana Grove
Indian Industrial Training
School Haskell
2016

112 Roger Peet
Men Against Sexism
2021

113 Colin Matthes
Muhammad Ali
2004

114 Susie Wilson
Octavia E. Butler
2019

115 Jenny Schmid
Int'l Ladies' Garment Workers
Union
2019

116 Rocky Dobey
Prison Justice Day
2010

117 Josh MacPhee
Sacco / Vanzetti
2010

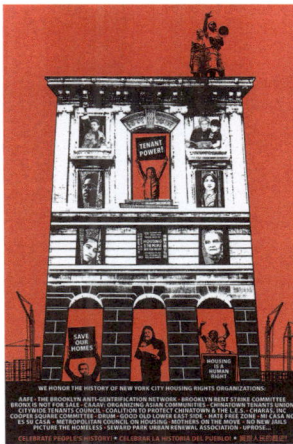

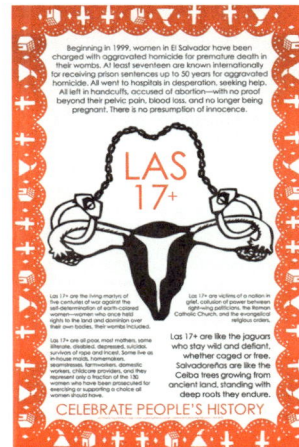

118 Jennifer Cartwright
     ADAPT
     2006

119 Janet Attard
     Major Taylor
     2012

120 Shannon Gerard, Mary Tremonte
     Corita Kent
     2017

121 Miriam Klein Stahl
     Funmilayo Ransome Kuti
     2020

122 Tomie Arai
     Tenant Power!
     2021

123 John Jennings
     The Funsten 500
     2021

124 Eli Brown
     Bayard Rustin
     2016

125 Camila Rosa
     Landless Workers' Movement
     2020

126 Mincho Vega
     Las 17+
     2018

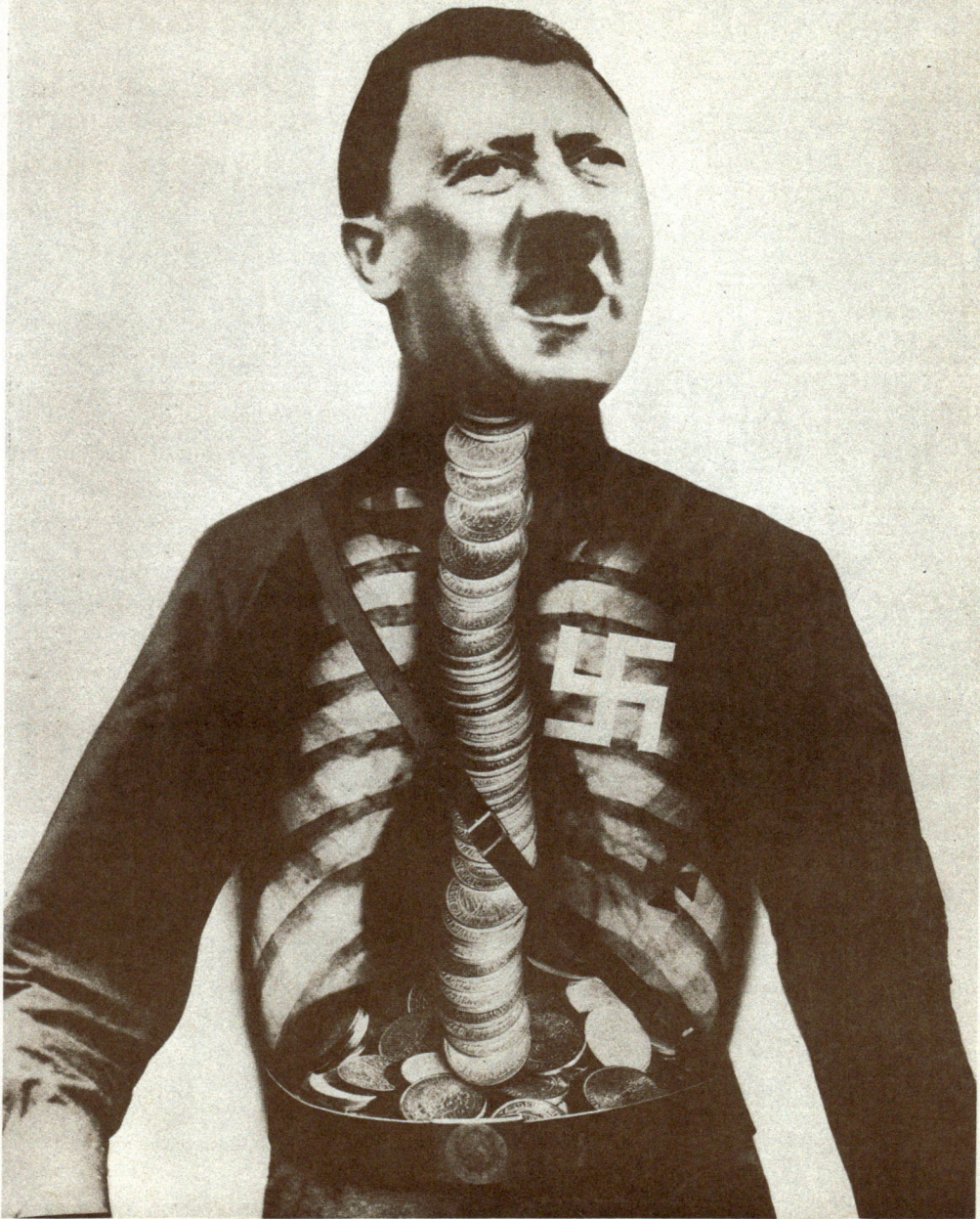

ADOLF, DER ÜBERMENSCH: **Schluckt Gold und redet Blech**

127   John Heartfield
Adolf, der Übermensch:
Schluckt Gold und redet Blech
1932

128 Grapus, Les Graphistes Associés
[ohne Text – no text]
1990

Umweltschutz
Abrüstung

129   Anonym
Umweltschutz / Abrüstung
1979

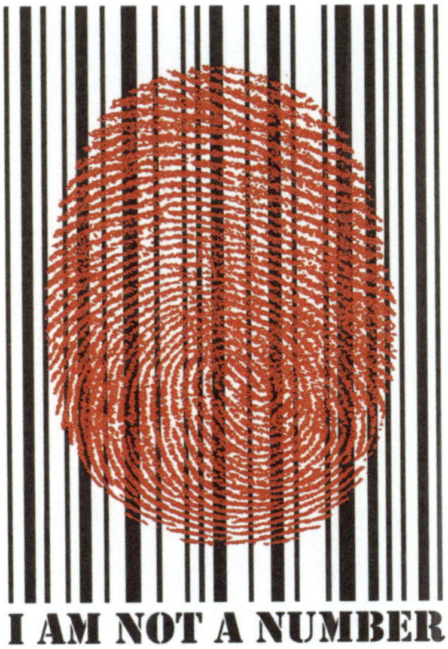

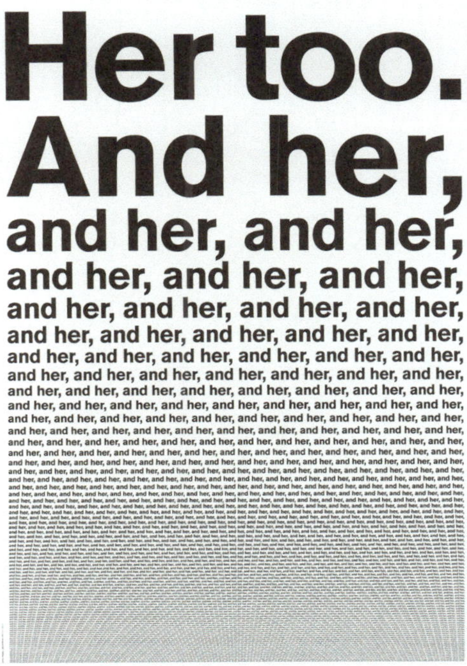

130 Studio Flex / Michael Speranza
Brainwash
2018

131 Armando Milani
I Am Not a Number
2008

132 Jean-Marc Seiler
Du bist Kaufkraft
1999

133 Lahav Halevy
Her Too. And Her, (…)
2017

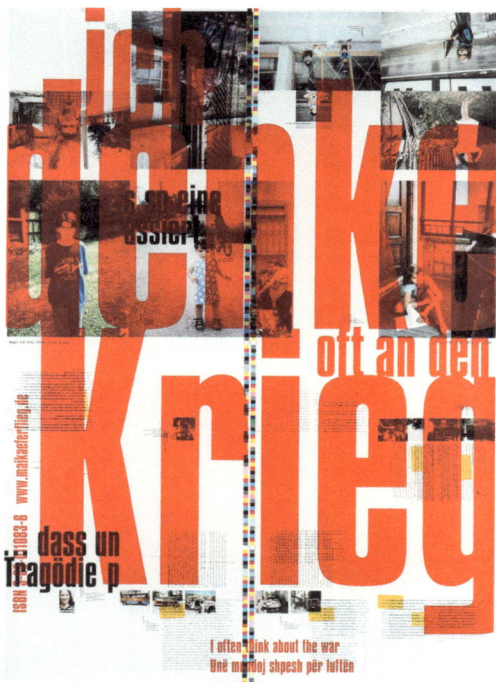

134   Piär Amrein
       Put Out Putin!
       2022

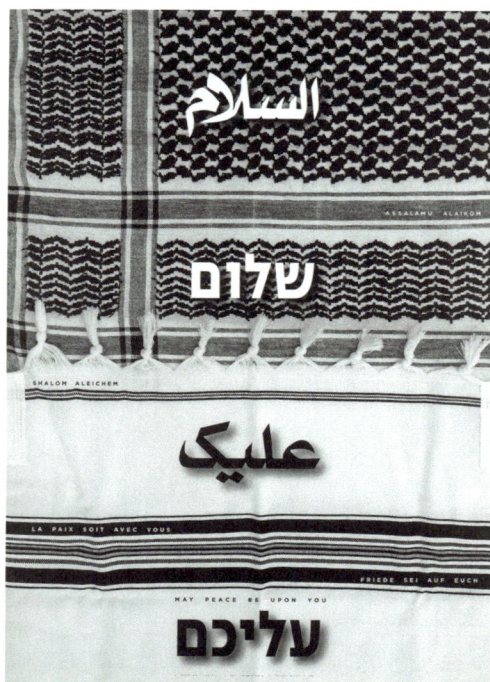

135   Anna Berkenbusch   136   Studio AND / Jean-Benoît Lévy
       Ich denke oft an den Krieg   Assalamu alaikom / Shalom aleichem
       2003   2015

Von Wut geformt:
Typografie in Protestplakaten

Silas Munro

Aktivistinnen und Aktivisten nutzen die Typografie seit jeher als wirkungsvolles Werkzeug des visuellen Protests, um auf verschiedene Arten der Unterdrückung aufmerksam zu machen. Ungleichheit wird in einer eindringlichen Formensprache vorgetragen, die noch die Spuren ihrer Gestalterinnen und Gestalter aufweist. Häufig erinnern die von Hand gefertigten und beschrifteten Schilder, Zeichen und Plakate an die Aktionen der Protestierenden. Die vielfältigen typografischen Umsetzungen in der Plakatsammlung des Museum für Gestaltung Zürich zeugen von ihrer starken Wirkungskraft in den Händen ausgebildeter Designerinnen und Designer und in alltäglichem Aktivismus. Diese Plakate tragen die Handschrift von Revolutionen und wurden von Demonstrierenden auf den Strassen weltweit hochgehalten oder aufgehängt. Die bedruckten Materialien dokumentieren die Geschichte der sozialen Bewegungen und des technologischen Wandels.

Seit den 1920er-Jahren und bis heute funktioniert Typografie in den Werken von Künstlerinnen und Künstlern wie John Heartfield und Chaz Maviyane-Davies wie eine eigene Bildsprache, entweder in Form von Schlagzeilen oder als aussagekräftige Bildunterschrift, um zu verdeutlichen, zu kontextualisieren, zu verstärken, zu kommentieren oder Spannung zu erzeugen. Dabei lassen sich grosse Unterschiede zwischen den Buchstabenformen erkennen, von der scharfen Kritik des Kunstkollektivs Atelier Populaire, das 1968 mit kühnem Handlettering energisch gegen die französische Regierung protestierte →4/29/31/33/69/70, bis zur klaren, ausschliesslich aus Versalien bestehenden Schrift des amerikanischen Grafikdesigners Herb Lubalin, der den Fotosatz von Werbeplakaten aus den 1970er-Jahren übernahm, um auf die politische Polarisierung aufmerksam zu machen →152. Rubylith und andere Werkzeuge, die die Handmade-Typografie des Atelier Populaire ermöglichten, verleihen den Lettern mit ihren sympathischen Texturen und symbolischen Illustrationen eine natürliche Wärme, die viele andere Protestgrafiken beeinflusst hat. Im New York der 1980er-Jahre eigneten sich die künstlerisch-aktivistischen Kollektive Gran Fury →85 und Guerrilla Girls →18 die grafische Sprache von Unternehmen an, um mit bitterer Ironie und sparsamer Komposition vulnerable Botschaften marginalisierter Menschen zu vermitteln. Zur gleichen Zeit nutzte der später an den Folgen von Aids verstorbene Künstler Keith Haring Schriftzüge, die von urbanen Graffitis und Comics inspiriert waren, um seinen Protest auszudrücken, etwa gegen die Apartheid in Südafrika →61.

Woman Life Liberty

#IranRevolution2022
#MahsaAmini

137 Studio Kat Rahmani /
Golnar Kat Rahmani
Woman Life Liberty
2022

Anger-Shaped Language: Typography in Protest Posters

Silas Munro

Activists have long employed typography as a powerful tool to challenge various forms of oppression through visual protest. Inequity is directly confronted with urgent formal language that leaves traces of its maker. Often handcrafted and hand-lettered signs, placards, and posters serve as a potent reminder of protesters' actions. The diverse range of typographic expressions in the Museum für Gestaltung Zürich's Poster Collection demonstrates powerful agency in the hands of trained designers and everyday activists. These posters carry the imprint of revolutions and were posted and held by demonstrators on streets across the world. They consist of printed materials that chart the history of social movements and technological changes.

From the 1920s to the 2020s, in the work of artists ranging from John Heartfield to Chaz Maviyane-Davies, typography has operated as a form of imagery, either in headline form or as an essential caption to clarify, give context to, enhance, annotate, or introduce tension. One sees great contrast in letterforms from the brash critiques of the 1968 art collective Atelier Populaire, which used bold hand lettering to express their urgent protest against the French government →4/29/31/33/69/70, to the crisp, all-capital typography of American art director Herb Lubalin, who usurped the language of 1970s photo-lettering advertising copy to comment on political polarization →152. Atelier Populaire's use of rubylith and other handmade typographic tools gives raw warmth to letterforms with sympathetic textures and symbolic illustrations, which have influenced many other protest graphics. In 1980s New York, the artist-activist collectives Gran Fury →85 and Guerrilla Girls→18 appropriated corporate graphic languages with stark irony and spare composition to present vulnerable messages from marginalized people. Simultaneously, the artist Keith Haring, who died of AIDS-related complications, used lettering inspired by urban graffiti and comic book lettering to protest a range of issues, including apartheid in South Africa →61.

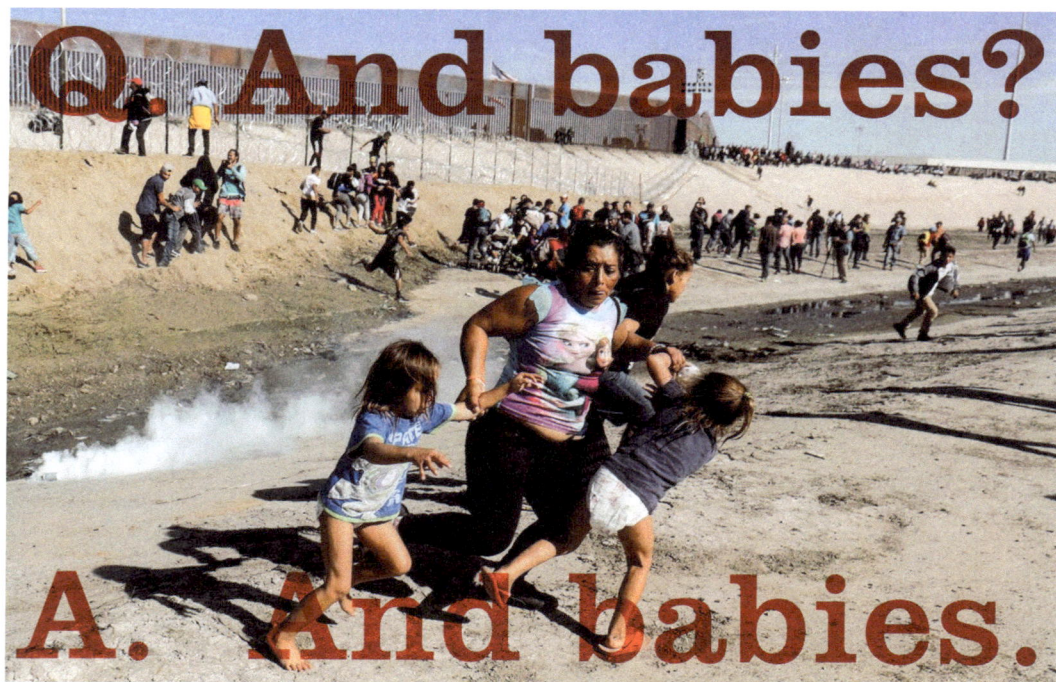

138   Frazier Dougherty, Jon Hendricks, Irving Petlin
       Q. And Babies? A. And Babies.
       1970

139   Plazm / Joshua Berger
       Q. And Babies? A. And Babies.
       2018

140   Yossi Lemel
      Israel Palestine 2002
      2002

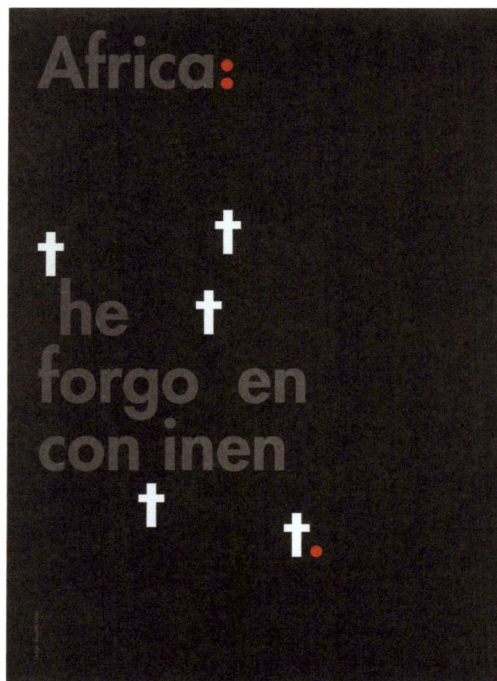

141   Paul Peter Piech
Soweto
1977

142   Anonym
Apartheid
ca. 1986

143   Armando Milani
Africa / The Forgotten Continent
2007

144   Niklaus Troxler
Capitalists of the World, Change!
2019

145 Gladys Acosta Ávila
Africa
1971

David King
Never Again! Stop the
Nazi National Front!
1978

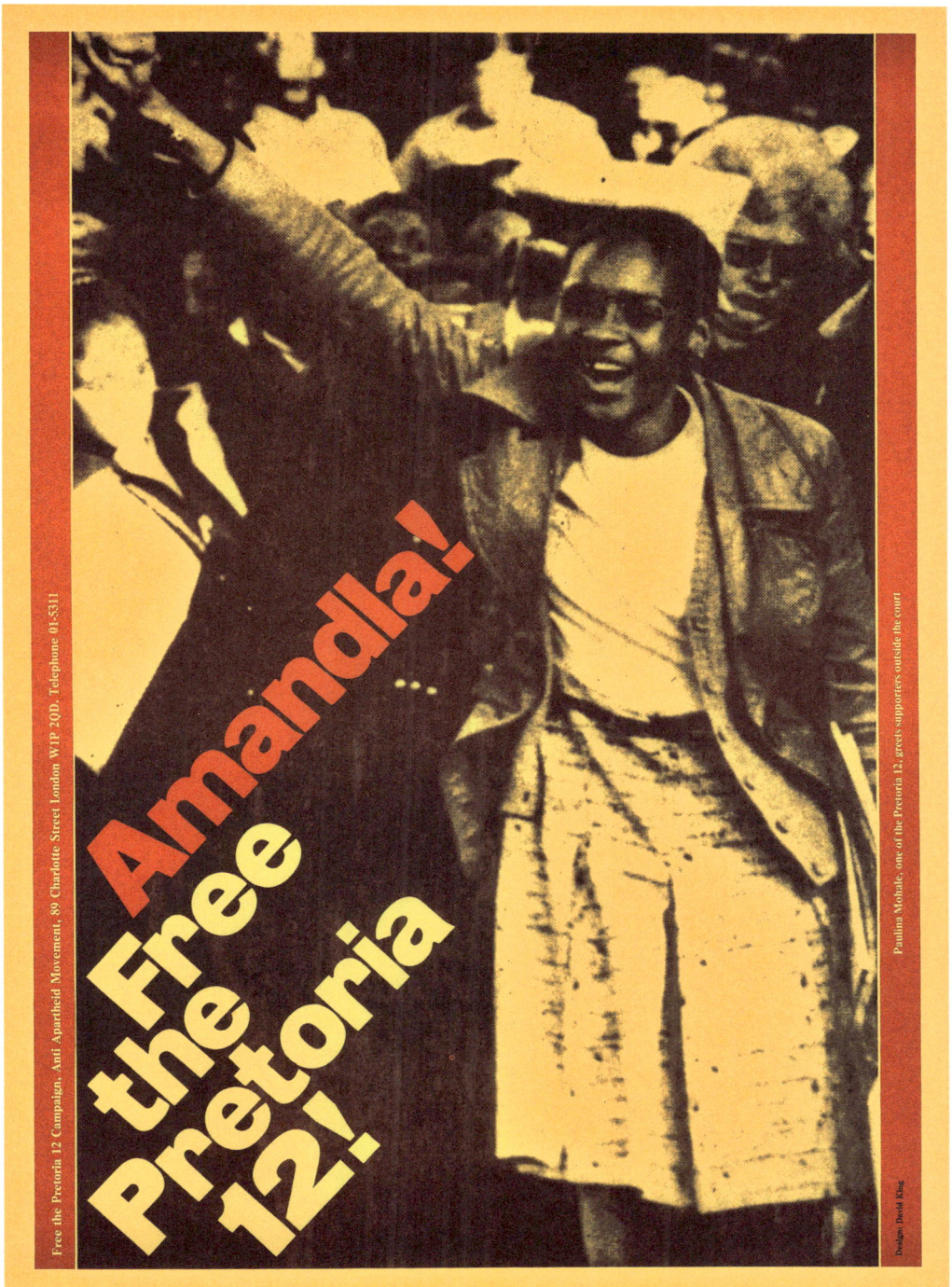

Free the Pretoria 12 Campaign, Anti Apartheid Movement, 89 Charlotte Street London W1P 2DD, Telephone 01-5311

Paulina Mohale, one of the Pretoria 12, greets supporters outside the court

Design: David King

147   David King
Amandla! Free the Pretoria 12!
1978

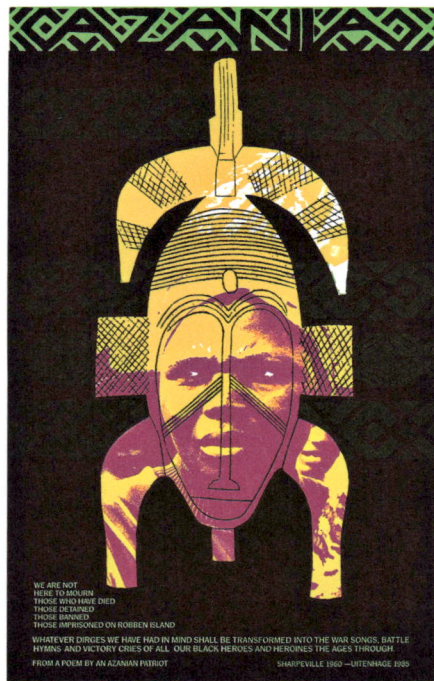

148   Luba Lukova
       War Crime
       1999

149   Grapus
       On va gagner!
       1991

150   Marlena Buczek Smith
       There Is No Victory in War
       2011

151   Fireworks Graphic Collective / Terry Forman
       Azania
       1985

THE NEXT WAR WILL DETERMINE NOT WHAT IS RIGHT BUT WHAT IS LEFT.

Paper: Karma Bright White, 80 lb. Cover by Potlatch Corporation, Northwest Paper Division & Andrews/Nelson/Whitehead. Printing: Trabon Printing, Kansas City, Missouri. Produced for the Herb Lubalin Study Center of Design and Typography at the Cooper Union. Illustration by Christoph Blumrich.

152 Herb Lubalin, Christopher Blumrich
The Next War Will Determine
Not What Is Right But What Is Left.
1972

153 Jean Carlu
Pour le désarmement des nations
1932

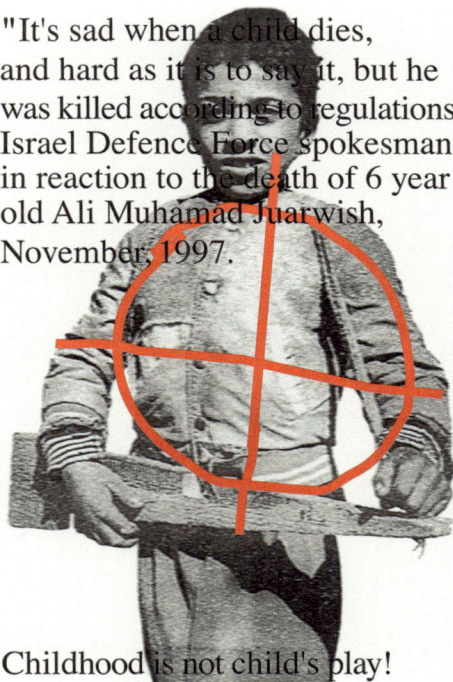

154 Mauro Bubbico
     Migranti / Diritti e pace
     2011

155 Josep Renau
     ¿Que haces tu para evitar esto?
     1937

156 Jānis Reinbergs
     Lūk, tava seja, Amerika!
     1972

157 David Tartakover
     Childhood Is Not Child's Play!
     1998

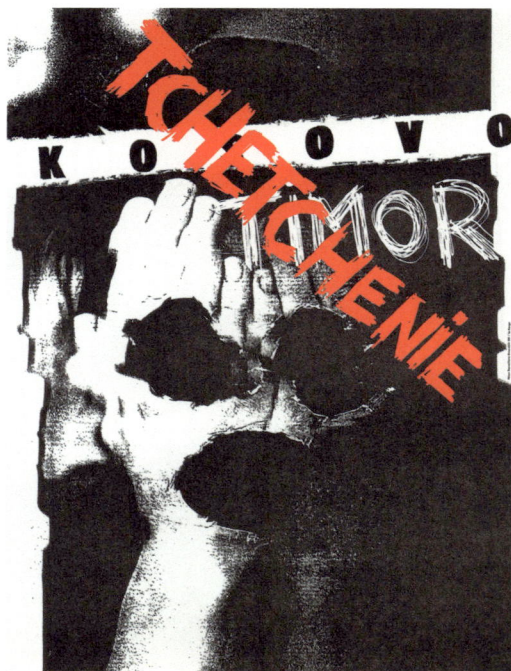

158   John Heartfield
Niemals wieder!
1932

159   stettlerbros. / Christoph Stettler
Ukruine
2015

160   Atelier Bundi / Stephan Bundi
Stoppt die Folter.
1985

161   Nous Travaillons Ensemble, NTE / Alex Jordan
Kosovo / Timor / Tchétchénie
2001

162   Steff Geissbühler
      Peace
      1985

Say that I was
a drum major
Say that I was
a drum major for justice
Say that I was
a drum major for peace
Say that I was
a drum major for
righteousness

Martin Luther King 1929–1968

Peter Gee Love Art Poster © 1968 HKL Ltd.

163 Peter Gee
Say That I Was a Drum Major
1968

UNITED COLORS
OF NETANYAHU.

ALL THOSE IN FAVOR OF THE
DEATH PENALTY, RAISE YOUR HAND.

As we see it, the United States is in with some pretty unseemly company. Isn't it time we took a firm
stand against the death penalty? To find out what you can do, call us. **AMNESTY INTERNATIONAL USA, 1-800-55AMNESTY**

164   David Tartakover
       United Colors of Netanyahu.
       1998

165   The Martin Agency / Jerry Torchia
       All Those in Favor of the Death Penalty,
       Raise Your Hand.
       1992

Peur
de vos
peurs

166 Intégral Ruedi Baur et associés / Ruedi Baur
Peur de vos peurs
ca. 2000

like
dislike

Anna Berkenbusch
Like / Dislike
2011

שלום

שנת השלושים לעצמאות ישראל ⬡

168   David Tartakover
Frieden – Peace
2000

Im Protestplakat sind Entwürfe einer besseren und gerechteren Welt
nur selten zu finden. Verbreiteter sind apokalyptische Bilder zerstörter Natur,
Bilder von der Gewalt des Menschen am Menschen. Werden sie im hedo-
nistischen Konsumumfeld plakatiert, provozieren sie und wollen emotional
schockieren. Sie konfrontieren die Betrachtenden unvermittelt mit einer
Realität, die gerne verharmlost oder verdrängt wird. Auf diese Weise wollen
sie ein Nachdenken, bestenfalls ein Engagement für eine andere Zukunft
anregen. Beispielhaft dafür steht das durch internationale Aktivistinnen
und Aktivisten Anfang 1970 global gestreute Plakat «Q. And Babies? A. And
Babies.» der Art Workers' Coalition →138. Es zeigt eine Fotografie des von
US-Soldaten am 16. März 1968 verübten Massakers im vietnamesischen
Dorf My Lai. Das Plakat wurde zur Anklage des Vietnamkriegs schlechthin
und beeinflusste den Umschwung der öffentlichen Meinung entscheidend.

Utopischen Darstellungen haftet häufig der Ruch der Weltfremdheit an.
Die kollektive Verbrüderung und Verschwesterung in intakter Landschaft
scheint verdächtig, der Flirt mit der Konsumwerbung gefährlich nah.
Zudem hat sich in der Geschichte des Widerstands allzu oft gezeigt, dass
diese Traumbilder in Eskapismus, gar ins Reaktionäre kippen können,
so beispielsweise bei einzelnen Reformbewegungen oder auch nationalen
Befreiungskämpfen. Eine ermächtigende Erfahrung von Kollektivität
und damit eine positive gesellschaftliche Vision drückt sich dagegen in den
Plakaten der 1998 von Josh MacPhee gegründeten Justseeds Artists'
Cooperative aus →109–126. Sie erzählen Geschichte von unten und widerset-
zen sich damit dem allgegenwärtigen Gefühl von Macht- und Hoffnungs-
losigkeit. Als visuelle transnationale Reise durch die Jahrzehnte wird von
erfolgreichem Protest und kreativem Aktivismus berichtet: ermutigende
Alltagsutopien ohne Realitätsflucht.

169 Henryk Tomaszewski
[ohne Text – no text]
1965

Visions of a better, more just world are rare in protest posters. More wide-spread are apocalyptic scenes of a devastated natural environment and violence against others. When posters are displayed in a hedonistic consumer environment, their goal is always to provoke and emotionally shock view-ers. People going about their daily activities are suddenly confronted with a reality that otherwise tends to be trivialized or suppressed. In this way, posters attempt to prompt reflection and, ideally, generate commitment to a different future. One example is the poster "Q. And Babies? A. And Babies.," created by the Art Workers' Coalition →138. Distributed globally by internation-al activists in early 1970, it shows a photograph of the massacre commit-ted by U.S. soldiers on March 16, 1968, in the Vietnamese village of My Lai. The poster gained fame as an iconic indictment of the Vietnam War and had a decisive influence on the shift in public opinion.

Utopian depictions often have a whiff of naivety. The ideal of a collective brotherhood and sisterhood in an intact landscape seems suspicious, and it comes dangerously close to flirting with consumer advertising. Moreover, the history of resistance has shown all too often that such dreamy-eyed images can become a form of escapism and even verge on the reactionary – as can be seen in certain reform movements and national liberation strug-gles. In contrast, the posters of the Justseeds Artists' Cooperative →109–126, founded in 1998 by Josh MacPhee, express the empowering experience of collectivity and thus a positive vision of society. They recount history from the bottom up, defying omnipresent feelings of powerlessness and hope-lessness. As a visual transnational journey through the decades, they document successful protests and creative activism. They present hopeful everyday utopias that do not attempt to escape reality.

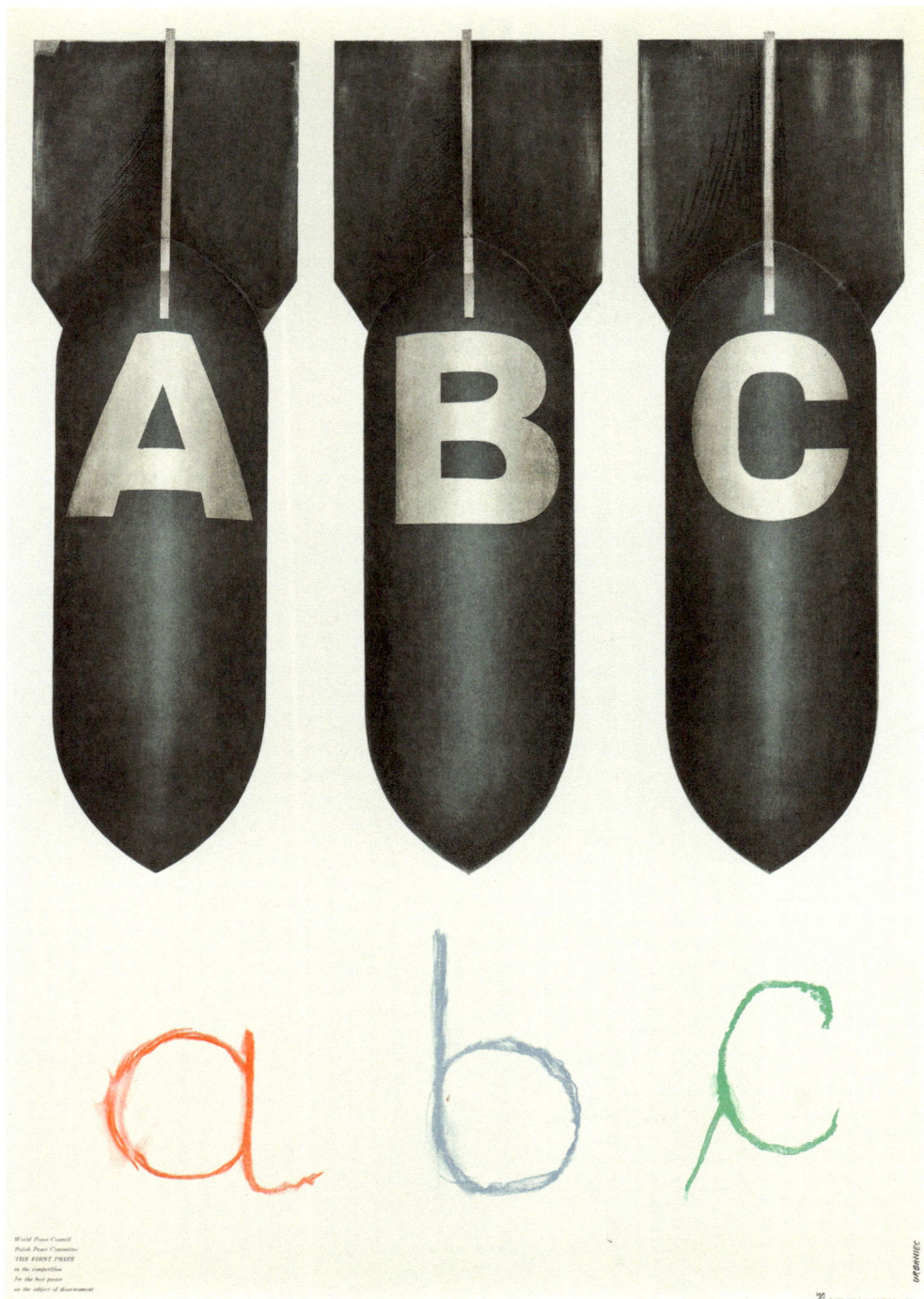

World Peace Council
Polish Peace Committee
THE FIRST PRIZE
in the competition
for the best poster
on the subject of disarmament

170 Maciej Urbaniec
A B C / a b c
1971

"IDEOLOGICAL COVERUP"

BRUCE KAIPER 1974

171   Bruce Kaiper
      Love
      1974

Alle abgebildeten Plakate stammen aus der Plakatsammlung des Museum für Gestaltung Zürich.
Die Rechte (insbesondere Urheberrechte) liegen bei
den Urheberinnen und Urhebern bzw. den Rechts-
nachfolgerinnen und -nachfolgern.

© 2025, ProLitteris, Zurich: Jean Carlu, Roman Ciéslewicz,
John Heartfield, Klaus Staeck, Niklaus Troxler
David King © The Estate of David King
Paul Peter Piech © The Estate of Paul Peter Piech
Hendryk Tomaszewski © Filip Pagowski
Tomi Ungerer (37, 39) © 1994, 1998 Diogenes
Verlag AG Zürich
Tomi Ungerer (40, 44) © Tomi Ungerer Estate /
Diogenes Verlag AG Zürich. All rights reserved.
Musée Tomi Ungerer – Centre international
de l'illustration

Die Daten des Katalogs folgen den Rubriken Gestaltung,
Plakattext, Erscheinungsjahr, Erscheinungsland,
Drucktechnik, Format und Donationsnachweis. Dabei
gelten insbesondere folgende Regelungen:

Plakattext: Die beste Textwiedergabe bildet die Abbil-
dung des Plakats selbst. Darum wird hier eine
vereinfachte Form wiedergegeben, welche nur die
aussagekräftigen Textbestandteile berücksichtigt.
Allfällige Umstellungen dienen der Verständlichkeit.
Das Zeichen / trennt inhaltliche Texteinheiten.
Jeweils in Klammern nachgestellt folgt die deutsche
und/oder englische Übersetzung.

Erscheinungsland: Das Erscheinungsland wird mit dem
international gebräuchlichen ISO-Code angegeben.

Format: Die Angaben werden in der Abfolge
Höhe × Breite und in Zentimetern gemacht. Weil die
Plakate oft nicht exakt rechtwinklig geschnitten
sind, werden die Abmessungen auf halbe Zentimeter
aufgerundet.

Donationsnachweis: Die Geschichte der Plakatsammlung geht auf das Jahr 1875 zurück. Angaben
zur Herkunft der Plakate sind in vielen Fällen nicht
überliefert. Erst in jüngerer Zeit werden Donatorinnen
und Donatoren von Plakaten – Institutionen oder
Einzelpersonen – konsequent festgehalten und in
Veröffentlichungen namentlich publiziert.

Die Plakatgeschichte ist ein junges Forschungsgebiet –
verlässliche Hinweise sind rar. Jeder Hinweis und
jede Ergänzung sind willkommen:
sammlung@museum-gestaltung.ch

All posters reproduced are from the Museum für
Gestaltung Zürich's Poster Collection. The copyrights
are held by the authors or their legal successors.

© 2025, ProLitteris, Zurich: Jean Carlu, Roman Ciéslewicz,
John Heartfield, Klaus Staeck, Niklaus Troxler
David King © The Estate of David King
Paul Peter Piech © The Estate of Paul Peter Piech
Hendryk Tomaszewski © Filip Pagowski
Tomi Ungerer (37, 39) © 1994, 1998 Diogenes
Verlag AG Zurich
Tomi Ungerer (40, 44) © Tomi Ungerer Estate /
Diogenes Verlag AG Zurich. All rights reserved.
Musée Tomi Ungerer – Centre international
de l'illustration

The data listed in the catalog is broken down into the
following sections: designer, poster title and/or text,
year and country of first appearance, printing technique,
size, and donor. In particular, the following rules have
been applied:

Poster text: The poster itself provides the best version
of the text, and thus a simplified form is used which
provides only the most meaningful elements. Any re-
arrangements that have been made are for purposes
of intelligibility. A slash separates textual units by con-
tent. The German and/or English translation is set in
parentheses after the poster text.

Country of first appearance: The country of first
appearance is identified by the internationally accepted
ISO code.

Format: The dimensions are given in centimeters as
height × width. Because posters are often not cut
exactly at right angles, the dimensions are rounded
off to the half-centimeter.

Donor: The history of the Poster Collection goes back to
1875. In many cases, we lack specific information
concerning the sources of posters in the collection.
Only recently have institutional or individual con-
tributors of posters been recorded consistently and
specified in our publications.

The history of posters is a recent field of research –
reliable information is rare. Any further references
or additional materials are welcome:
sammlung@museum-gestaltung.ch

1 Käthe Kollwitz (1867–1945)
Nie wieder Krieg / Mitteldeutscher
Jugendtag Leipzig (Never
Again War / Central German
Youth Day Leipzig)
1924 DE Lithografie – Lithograph
94 × 71,5 cm

2 David Tartakover (*1944)
Photo: Jim Hollander (*1949)
"Mother" / Images Internationales
pour les Droits de l'Homme et
du Citoyen («Mutter» / Internationales Bildmaterial für Menschen-
und Bürgerrechte – "Mother" /
International Visual Material for
Human and Civil Rights)
1987 IL Offset 84 × 59,5 cm
Donation David Tartakover

3 Plazm / Joshua Berger (*1967),
Peter Le
[ohne Text – no text]
2016 US Digitaldruck –
Digital print 36 × 27,5 cm
Donation Joshua Berger

4 Atelier Populaire
L'ordre règne (Hier herrscht
Ordnung – Order Prevails Here)
1968 FR Siebdruck – Screenprint
55,5 × 43 cm

5 David King (1943–2016)
Apartheid in Practice /
Law & Order in South Africa /
The political organisations
of the Black majority have been
banned and non-racial political
organisations are illegal (…)
(Apartheid in der Praxis / Recht
und Ordnung in Südafrika /
Die politischen Organisationen
der Schwarzen Mehrheit wurden
verboten, und nicht nach Ethnien
getrennte politische Organisationen sind illegal (…))
1978 GB Siebdruck – Screenprint
64,5 × 45 cm
Donation Richard Hollis

6 Luba Lukova (*1960)
Sudan
1999 US Siebdruck – Screenprint
100 × 69,5 cm
Donation Luba Lukova

7 Marlena Buczek Smith (*1977)
Abolish Torture
(Schafft die Folter ab)
2007 US Giclée-Druck –
Giclée print 86,5 × 61 cm
Donation Marlena Buczek Smith

8 Tomaso Marcolla (*1964)
Welcome (Willkommen)
2011 (Nachdruck – Reprint 2024)
IT Digitaldruck – Digital print
70 × 50 cm
Donation Tomaso Marcolla

9 Jean-Claude Matthey
Maroc: Comité de lutte contre
la répression au Maroc (Marokko:
Ausschuss zur Bekämpfung
der Repression in Marokko –
Morocco: Committee to Combat
Repression in Morocco)
ca. 1980 FR Siebdruck –
Screenprint 92 × 65 cm

10 Anonym
Internationaler Solidaritätskongress mit dem arabischen Volk
und mit Palästina (International
Solidarity Congress with the Arab
People and Palestine)
1979 PT Offset 39,5 × 28 cm

11 Ryan Slone (*1978)
No Other Choice / Globally, 68.5
million people have been uprooted
due to forced migration, often
caused by war and conflict. This is
one person every two seconds.
(Keine andere Wahl / 68,5 Millionen Menschen wurden welt-
weit durch Zwangsmigration aus
ihrer Heimat vertrieben, oft auf-
grund von Kriegen und Konflikten.
Das ist ein Mensch alle zwei
Sekunden.)
2016 (Nachdruck – Reprint 2022)
US Inkjet 91 × 60,5 cm
Donation Ryan Slone

12 Chaz Maviyane-Davies (*1952)
Palestine: A Homeland Denied
(Palästina: ein verwehrtes
Heimatland)
1980 ZW Offset 57,5 × 42 cm
Donation Chaz Maviyane-Davies

13 Juan R. Fuentes (*1950)
Mexico
2015 ES Offset 99 × 68 cm
Donation Un Mundo Feliz,
UMF, Madrid

14 Goodall Integrated Design /
Derwyn Goodall (*1960)
A rising toll of protesters have been
killed by Iranian authorities
since demonstrations triggered
by the death of Mahsa Jina Amini,
who was arrested and then
later died in police custody. (…)
(Seit den Unruhen, die durch
den Tod von Mahsa Jina Amini,
die festgenommen wurde und
später in Polizeigewahrsam
starb, ausgelöst wurden, ist die
Zahl der von iranischen Behörden
getöteten Demonstrierenden
gestiegen. (…))
2023 CA Digitaldruck – Digital print
71,5 × 56,5 cm
Donation Derwyn Goodall

15 Savaş Çekiç (*1960)
Bedenimiz bizim
(Unsere Körper gehören uns –
Our Bodies Belong to Us)
1998 TR Siebdruck – Screenprint
69,5 × 48 cm
Donation Savaş Çekiç

16 Jeannie Friedman (*1948)
Women Unite!
(Frauen, vereinigt euch!)
1976 US Siebdruck – Screenprint
52 × 45 cm
Donation Jeannie Friedman

17 Vanessa Vérillon (*1970)
Journée internationale des droits
des femmes / 8 mars 2005
(Weltfrauentag / 8. März 2005 –
International Women's Day /
March 8, 2005)
2005 FR Siebdruck – Screenprint
176 × 120 cm

18 Guerrilla Girls
Guerrilla Girls Demand a Return
to Traditional Values on Abortion.
Before the mid-19th century,
abortion in the first few months
of pregnancy was legal. Even
the Catholic Church did not forbid
it until 1869. (Die Guerrilla Girls
fordern beim Thema Abtreibung
eine Rückkehr zu traditionellen
Werten. Vor der Mitte des 19. Jahrhunderts war Abtreibung in den
ersten Monaten der Schwanger-
schaft legal. Selbst die katholi-
sche Kirche verbot sie erst 1869.)
1992 US Offset 43,5 × 56 cm

19 Garage Graphix,
Talking Posters Project
I had this big image that I was
tough and no-one was game to
say anything to me about it ……
But there's dykes all over the
place and I don't need that cover
now. (Ich hatte dieses Image,
dass ich tough bin und niemand
sich traut, mir was zu sagen ……
Aber es gibt überall Lesben,
und ich brauche diese Fassade
jetzt nicht mehr.)
1985 AU Siebdruck – Screenprint
72,5 × 49 cm

20 Fireworks Graphic Collective /
Terry Forman
Our Bodies, Our Lives, Our Right
to Decide / Abortion without
Apology – We Won't Go Back!
(Unsere Körper, unser Leben,
unsere Entscheidung / Abtreibung
ohne Entschuldigung – Wir gehen
nicht zurück!)
1989 US Offset 64 × 48,5 cm

21 See Red Women's Workshop
So Long as Women Are Not Free
the People Are Not Free
(Solange Frauen nicht frei sind,
sind Menschen nicht frei)
1978 GB Siebdruck – Screenprint
65,5 × 53 cm

22 Fireworks Graphic Collective /
Terry Forman
Down with the Chilean Dictatorship! Support the Popular
Resistance! (Nieder mit der chilenischen Diktatur! Unterstützt
den Widerstand des Volkes!)
1983 US Siebdruck – Screenprint
52 × 44,5 cm

23 Atelier de Création Graphique /
Pierre Bernard (1942–2015),
Grégoire Romanet (*1973)
Contre les violences
faites aux femmes (Nein zur
Gewalt gegen Frauen –
No to Violence against Women)
2004 FR Siebdruck – Screenprint
168 × 119 cm
Donation Pierre Bernard

24 Gérard Paris-Clavel (*1943)
Qui a peur d'une femme?
(Wer hat Angst vor einer Frau? –
Who Is Afraid of a Woman?)
1997 FR Siebdruck – Screenprint
120 × 81 cm

25 Asamblea de Artistas Revolucionarios de Oaxaca (ASARO)
Cuando una mujer avanza …
no hay hombre que la detenga
(Kein Mann kann eine Frau
aufhalten, die ihren Weg geht –
No Man Can Stop a Woman
Who Goes Her Own Way)
2007 (Nachdruck – Reprint 2017)
MX Hochdruck – Letterpress
59,5 × 80 cm

26 San Francisco Poster Brigade /
Rachael Romero (*1953)
Stop Forced Sterilization /
Public Hearings on Sterilization
(Zwangssterilisationen stoppen /
Öffentliche Anhörungen zum
Thema Sterilisation)
1977 US Offset 57,5 × 44,5 cm
Donation Rachael Romero

27 San Francisco Poster Brigade /
Rachael Romero (*1953)
Del Monte Profits from Apartheid /
Support the Liberation Struggle /
Boycott All Del Monte Products
(Del Monte profitiert von
der Apartheid / Unterstützt den
Befreiungskampf / Boykottiert
alle Produkte von Del Monte)
ca. 1977 US Offset 57,5 × 45 cm
Donation Rachael Romero

28 San Francisco Poster Brigade /
Rachael Romero (*1953)
Boycott Nestlé / For Unethical
Promotion and Sale of Infant
Formula in the Third World /
Genocide for Profit (Boykottiert
Nestlé / Wegen unethischer
Werbung und Verkauf von
Säuglingsnahrung in der Dritten
Welt / Völkermord aus Profitgier)
1979 US Offset 59 × 45 cm
Donation Rachael Romero

29 Atelier Populaire
Frontières = répression
(Grenzen = Repression –
Borders = Repression)
1968 FR Siebdruck – Screenprint
73,5 × 59 cm
Donation Urs Roland Berger

30 Atelier Populaire
[ohne Text – no text]
1968 FR Siebdruck – Screenprint
122,5 × 85,5 cm

31 Atelier Populaire
L'état c'est moi (Der Staat,
das bin ich – The State Is Me)
1968 FR Siebdruck – Screenprint
84 × 58 cm

32 Alain Le Quernec (*1944)
Attention / Au début Hitler faisait
rire (Vergiss nicht: Hitler wurde
am Anfang auch nicht ernst
genommen – Don't forget: they
did not take Hitler seriously
at the beginning either)
1987 FR Siebdruck – Screenprint
88 × 62 cm

33 Atelier Populaire
On vous intoxique! (Man vergiftet
euch! – You Are Being Poisoned!)
1968 FR Siebdruck – Screenprint
84 × 79 cm

34 Nous travaillons ensemble /
Alex Jordan (*1947)
La France me mérite-t-elle?
Papa et Maman sont des
« immigrés ». (…) (Ist Frankreich
meiner würdig? Ich bin das
Kind von «Einwanderern». (…) –
Is France worthy of me? I am
the child of "immigrants." (…))
1993 FR Offset 85 × 60 cm

35 Grapus
Rich / Poor (Reich / Arm)
1989 FR Siebdruck – Screenprint
84 × 59,5 cm

36 Larry Dunst
Photo: Steve Horn (*1932)
I Want Out (Ich will raus)
1971 US Offset 102 × 76 cm

37 Tomi Ungerer (1931–2019)
Join the Free and Fat Society
(Werde Teil der freien
und fetten Gesellschaft)
1967 US Offset 59 × 73,5 cm

38 Victore Design Works /
James Victore (*1962)
Disney Go Home
(Disney, geh nach Hause)
ca. 1997 US Siebdruck –
Screenprint 96,5 × 63,5 cm

39 Tomi Ungerer (1931–2019)
Eat (Iss)
1967 US Offset 68,5 × 53,5 cm

40 Tomi Ungerer (1931–2019)
Kiss for Peace (Friedenskuss)
1967 US Offset 55,5 × 70 cm

41 Fons Hickmann m23 /
Fons Hickmann (*1966)
Stop the Death Penalty in USA!
Amnesty International
(Stoppt die Todesstrafe in den
USA! Amnesty International)
2010 DE Digitaldruck –
Digital print 118,5 × 84 cm
Donation Fons Matthias
Hickmann

42 Design Is Play / Mark Fox (*1961),
Angie Wang (*1970)
Trump
2016 US Prägedruck –
Embossed print 57,5 × 48,5 cm
Donation Design Is Play,
San Francisco

43 U. G. Sato (*1935)
Non aux essais nucléaires
(Nein zu Atomtests! –
No to Nuclear Testing)
1995 JP Siebdruck – Screenprint
174,5 × 118,5 cm
Donation U. G. Sato

44 Tomi Ungerer (1931–2019)
The Americans Are Coming
(Die Amerikaner kommen)
1967 US Offset 68,5 × 53,5 cm

45 Alejandro Magallanes (*1971)
Ciudad Juárez / 300 mujeres
muertas / 500 mujeres
desaparecidas (Ciudad Juárez /
300 Femizide / 500 ver-
schwundene Frauen – Ciudad
Juárez / 300 Femicides /
500 Disappeared Women)
2003 MX Siebdruck – Screenprint
93 × 68 cm
Donation Alejandro Magallanes

46 Pedro Yamashita (*1947)
Peace / Messages to
the World in the 21st Century
(Frieden / Botschaften an
die Welt im 21. Jahrhundert)
2001 JP Siebdruck – Screenprint
119 × 84 cm
Donation Pedro Yamashita

47 Victore Design Works /
James Victore (*1962)
Racism and the Death Penalty /
Double Justice / _ _ gg _ r
(Rassismus und Todesstrafe /
Doppelbestrafung / _ _ g _ r)
1993 US Offset 82,5 × 59 cm

48 Anonym
[ohne Text – no text]
ca. 1973 Offset 80 × 61 cm

49 Niklaus Troxler (*1947)
[Tote Bäume – Dead Trees]
1992 CH Siebdruck – Screenprint
128 × 90,5 cm
Donation Niklaus Troxler

50 Luba Lukova (*1960)
Eco Crime (Umweltverbrechen)
1999 US Siebdruck – Screenprint
90,5 × 63 cm
Donation Luba Lukova

51 Victore Design Works /
James Victore (*1962)
25 Years / Earth Day / 1970–1995
(25 Jahre / Tag der Erde /
1970–1995)
1995 US Siebdruck – Screenprint
99 × 69 cm

52 Asamblea de Artistas Revolucio-
narios de Oaxaca (ASARO)
Reformas energetica educativa
financiera electoral laboral
(Reformen im Energiesektor, im
Bildungsbereich, im Bereich
Finanzen, Wahlen und Arbeit –
Reforms in the Energy,
Education, and Finance Sectors,
Elections and Labor)
2015 (Nachdruck – Reprint 2017)
MX Hochdruck – Letterpress
120 × 81,5 cm

53 Elisabetta Carboni (*1950)
Lavoratori, lavoratrici, studenti,
sosteniamo con la nostra
presenza i pescatori di Cabras
ingiustamente processati
(Arbeiter, Arbeiterinnen, Studie-
rende, mit unserer Präsenz
unterstützen wir die zu Unrecht
verurteilten Fischer von Cabras –
Workers, students, with our
presence we support the unjustly
condemned fishers of Cabras)
1972 IT Hochdruck – Letterpress
100 × 70 cm

54 Piär Amrein (*1957)
Mehr für die Reichen /
Meer für die Armen (More
for the Rich / Sea for the Poor)
2015 CH Hochdruck –
Letterpress 52 × 24,5 cm
Donation Piär Amrein

55 Götz Gramlich (*1974),
Klaus Staeck (*1938)
[ohne Text – no text]
2014 DE Offset 84,5 × 59,5 cm
Donation Götz Gramlich,
Klaus Staeck

56 Gérard Paris-Clavel (*1943)
Pas d'achat, pas de bonheur
(Ohne Shoppen kein Glück –
No Shopping, No Happiness)
2002 FR Siebdruck – Screenprint
175 × 118,5 cm

57 Agil / Sascha Lobe (*1967)
Die Würde des Menschen
ist *un*antastbar
(Human Dignity Is *In*violable)
1993 DE Offset 71 × 50 cm

58 Gérard Paris-Clavel (*1943)
Money World (Geld Welt)
1992 FR Siebdruck – Screenprint
160 × 120 cm

59 Klaus Staeck (*1938)
Nord-Süd-Gefälle
(North–South Divide)
1991 DE Offset 84 × 59 cm

60 Sigel Shimo'Oka (*1949)
Photo: Seiji Yamada
African Break-Fast.
(Afrikanisches Frühstück.)
1997 JP Offset 103,5 × 73 cm
Donation Sigel Shimo'Oka

61 Keith Haring (1958–1990)
Free South Africa
(Freiheit für Südafrika)
1985 US Offset 122 × 122 cm

62 Anonym
¡Cese! (Es muss aufhören! –
It Has to Stop!)
1986 CU Siebdruck – Screenprint
74,5 × 49 cm

63 Reto Coaz (*1975)
Plakate gegen das WEF /
Modell Davos.05 /
World Economic Forum
(Posters against WEF /
Model Davos.05 / World
Economic Forum)
2004 CH Offset 60 × 42 cm
Donation Urs Gägauf

64 Ulrike Würfel (*1990)
Afrika / Afrika / Afrika (…)
2016 DE Offset 84,5 × 59,5 cm
Donation Götz Gramlich

65 Asela Maria Pérez (1934–2006)
Jornada internacional de solida-
ridad con America Latina
(Internationale Solidaritäts-
woche mit Lateinamerika –
International Week of Solidarity
with Latin America)
1968 CU Offset 54,5 × 33 cm

66 Atelier Populaire
Laissons la peur du rouge aux
bêtes à cornes (Die Angst vor den
Roten sollten wir dem Hornvieh
überlassen – Fear of the Reds
Should Be Left to Horned Cattle)
1968 FR Siebdruck – Screenprint
33 × 43,5 cm

67 Grapus
Picasso 28.12.1961 /
Grapus 28.12.1987
1987 FR Offset 60 × 80 cm
Donation François Chalet

68 Piotr Młodozeniec (*1956)
Coexist / Coexistence
(Koexistieren / Koexistenz)
2000 PL, IL Siebdruck –
Screenprint 70 × 100 cm
Donation Piotr Młodozeniec

69 Atelier Populaire
Non (Nein – No)
1968 FR Siebdruck – Screenprint
61 × 42,5 cm

70 Atelier Populaire
La lutte continue (Der Kampf geht
weiter – The Fight Continues)
1968 FR Siebdruck – Screenprint
28 × 44,5 cm

71 Stefano Rovai (*1958)
31:1:2000 / Fuoriuscita di cianuro
da una vasca della miniera d'oro di
Aurul Romania / La sostanza
tossica si è riversata nel fiume
Tibisco e da qui nel Danubio.
È la più grande catastrofe ecolo-
gica in Europa dopo Chernobyl.
(31.1.2000 / Austritt von Cyanid
aus einem Staubecken der
Aurul-Goldmine in Rumänien /
Das Gift hat sich in die Theiss
und von dort in die Donau ergos-
sen. Nach Tschernobyl die grösste
Umweltkatastrophe Europas. –
Jan. 31, 2000 / Cyanide leaked
from a reservoir at the Aurul gold
mine in Romania. / The poison
spilled into the River Tisza and
from there into the Danube.
The biggest environmental disaster
in Europe since Chernobyl.)
2000 IT Siebdruck – Screenprint
70,5 × 50,5 cm
Donation Stefano Rovai

72 Atelier Bagarre /
Hakim Abel Ben Youcef (*1977)
Paris / 2024 / Control
(Paris / 2024 / Kontrolle)
2023 FR Offset 42 × 30 cm
Donation Hakim Abel Ben Youcef

73 Naoki Hirai (*1960)
Is Your Baby Safe? Save Your Child
from the Polluted Water. (Ist dein
Baby sicher? Schütze dein Kind vor
verseuchtem Wasser.)
2001 JP Offset 103 × 73 cm
Donation Naoki Hirai

74 Anonym
Am 26. April 1986 explodierte
im Atomkraftwerk von Tschernobyl ein Reaktorblock. Dabei
wurden grosse Mengen an radio-
aktivem Material freigesetzt.
Das Gebiet wurde unbewohnbar
und die langfristigen Konse-
quenzen für Mensch und Umwelt
waren katastrophal. (…)
(On April 26, 1986, a reactor block
exploded at the Chernobyl
nuclear power plant. Large quan-
tities of radioactive material
were released. The area became
uninhabitable and the long-
term consequences for people
and the environment were
catastrophic. (…))
2011 CH Hochdruck – Letterpress
64 × 45 cm

75 Piär Amrein (*1957)
Terracotta
2019 Hochdruck – Letterpress
46 × 31 cm
Donation Piär Amrein

76 Klaus Staeck (*1938)
Coca-Cola präsentiert
(Coca-Cola Presents)
1994 DE Offset 84 × 59 cm

77 Marlena Buczek Smith (*1977)
[ohne Text – no text]
2009 US Giclée-Druck –
Giclée print 86 × 61 cm
Donation Marlena Buczek Smith

78 Shigeo Fukuda (1932–2009)
Victory 1945 (Sieg 1945)
1975 JP Offset 97,5 × 67,5 cm

79 Savaş Çekiç (*1960)
[ohne Text – no text]
1998 TR Offset 69 × 48 cm
Donation Savaş Çekiç

80 Tomaso Marcolla (*1964)
[ohne Text – no text]
2015 (Nachdruck – Reprint 2024)
MX Digitaldruck – Digital print
70 × 50 cm
Donation Tomaso Marcolla

81 Lex Drewinski (*1951)
Racism (Rassismus)
1993 DE Siebdruck – Screenprint
70 × 100 cm

82 Chaz Maviyane-Davies (*1952)
Globalisation (Globalisierung)
2005 (Nachdruck – Reprint 2015)
ES Offset 99 × 68 cm
Donation Un Mundo Feliz,
UMF, Madrid

83 Victore Design Works /
James Victore (*1962)
Celebrate Columbus 1492–1992 /
América hoy, 500 años después /
America Today, 500 Years Later /
L'Amérique aujourd'hui,
500 ans plus tard (Amerika heute,
500 Jahre später)
1992 US Offset 90,5 × 60,5 cm

84 Lahav Halevy (*1965)
Syrian Killer (Syrischer Mörder)
2016 IL Offset 98,5 × 68,5 cm
Donation Lahav Halevy

85 Gran Fury
Aidsgate
1987 US Offset 80,5 × 60 cm

86 Robbie Conal (*1944)
Dough Nation
1997 US Offset 91,5 × 61 cm

87 Mauro Bubbico (*1957)
No Nuke / No Neo Dux (Keine
Nukleartechnik / Kein neuer Dux)
2011 IT Offset 97 × 67 cm
Donation Mauro Bubbico

88 Luis Balaguer
Jornada continental de apoyo a
Vietnam, Cambodia y Laos (Kon-
tinentaler Tag zur Unterstützung
für Vietnam, Kambodscha und
Laos – Continental Day in Support
of Vietnam, Cambodia, and Laos)
1969 CU Siebdruck – Screenprint
63,5 × 41,5 cm

89 Roman Cieślewicz (1930–1996)
CD / Corps diplomatique
(CD / Körper der Diplomatie –
Body of Diplomacy)
1994, Entwurf – Design 1974 PL
Siebdruck – Screenprint
100 × 70 cm

90 Swoon (*1977)
Celebrate People's History /
¡El Agua es nuestra carajo! (Feiert
die Geschichte der Menschen /
Das Wasser gehört uns, verdammt
noch mal! – The Water Is Ours,
Damnit!)
2005 US Offset 43,5 × 28 cm

91 Chip Thomas (*1957)
Celebrate People's History /
Sojourner Truth, born
Isabella (Belle) Baumfree,
c. 1797–November 26, 1883,
was an African-American
abolitionist and women's rights
activist. Truth was born into
slavery in Swartekill, NY, but escaped with her infant daughter
to freedom in 1826. (…) (Feiert die
Geschichte der Menschen /
Sojourner Truth, ca. 1797 geboren
als Isabella (Belle) Baumfree,
gestorben am 26.11.1883, war eine
afroamerikanische Sklaverei-
gegnerin und Frauenrechtlerin.
Als Sklavin in Swartekill, New York,
geboren, floh Truth 1826 mit
ihrer kleinen Tochter in die Freiheit. (…))
2021 US Offset 43,5 × 28 cm

92 Asamblea de Artistas Revolucio-
narios de Oaxaca (ASARO)
Muerte al capitalismo
(Tod dem Kapitalismus –
Death to Capitalism)
2007 (Nachdruck – Reprint 2017)
MX Hochdruck – Letterpress
40 × 61 cm

93 Asamblea de Artistas Revolucio-
narios de Oaxaca (ASARO)
¡Pueblo! ¡Defiende tu petróleo!
(Menschen! Kämpft um euer Öl! –
People! Fight for Your Oil!)
2007 (Nachdruck – Reprint 2017)
MX Hochdruck – Letterpress
80,5 × 60,5 cm

94 Nenad Cizl (*1980)
Got Oil? (Habt ihr Öl?)
2004 SI Inkjet 100 × 70,5 cm

95 Suunnittelutoimisto Both /
Timo Berry (*1973)
Photo: Timo Berry (*1973),
Ida Pimenoff (*1977)
Amnesty International / Poster
Designers for Amnesty: Freedom
of Expression (Amnesty Interna-
tional / Plakatgestalterinnen und
-gestalter für Amnesty: Recht
auf freie Meinungsäusserung)
2003 FI Offset 100 × 70 cm
Donation Timo Berry

96– Vincent Perrottet (*1958)
98 Photo: Vincent Perrottet (*1958)
On peut rêver. (Man wird ja
wohl träumen dürfen –
One Is Allowed to Dream)
2011 FR Siebdruck – Screenprint
80 × 60,5 cm
Donation Vincent Perrottet

99 Vincent Perrottet (*1958)
Et le respect ??
(Wo bleibt der Respekt?? –
Where Is the Respect??)
2011 FR Siebdruck – Screenprint
80 × 60,5 cm
Donation Vincent Perrottet

100 Gunter Rambow (*1938)
Deutschland den Deutschen /
Hamburg den Hamburgern /
Pinneberg den Pinnebergern /
Frau Strube der Frau Strube /
Rassismus macht einsam
(Germany for the Germans /
Hamburg for the Residents
of Hamburg / Pinneberg for the
Pinnebergers / Frau Strube
for Frau Strube / Racism Makes
Us Lonely)
1995 DE Offset 118,5 × 84 cm
Donation Gunter Rambow

101 Gunter Rambow (*1938)
Deutschland den Deutschen /
Bayern den Bayern / München
den Münchnern / Herr Huber dem
Herrn Huber / Fremdenangst
macht einsam (Germany for the
Germans / Bavaria for Bavarians /
Munich for the People of Munich /
Herr Huber for Herr Huber / Fear
of Foreigners Makes Us Lonely)
1995 DE Offset 118,5 × 84 cm
Donation Gunter Rambow

102 Gunter Rambow (*1938)
Deutschland den Deutschen /
Frankfurt den Frankfurtern /
Seckbach den Seckbachern /
Herr Meier dem Herrn Meier /
Rassismus macht einsam
(Germany for the Germans /
Frankfurt for the Residents of
Frankfurt / Seckbach for the
Seckbachers / Herr Meier for Herr
Meier / Racism Makes Us Lonely)
1995 DE Offset 118,5 × 84,5 cm
Donation Gunter Rambow

103 Gunter Rambow (*1938)
Deutschland den Deutschen /
Sachsen den Sachsen / Leipzig den
Leipzigern / Herr Wunderlich
dem Herrn Wunderlich / Fremden-
angst macht einsam (Germany
for the Germans / Saxony for the
Saxons / Leipzig for the Leipzi-
gers / Herr Wunderlich for Herr
Wunderlich / Fear of Foreigners
Makes Us Lonely)
1995 DE Offset 118,5 × 84,5 cm
Donation Gunter Rambow

104 Anonym
Libérez Angela Davis (Befreit
Angela Davis – Free Angela Davis)
ca. 1970 FR Siebdruck –
Screenprint 60 × 40 cm

105 Fons Hickmann m23 /
Fons Hickmann (*1966)
Woman Life Freedom / Hadis
Najafi / Shot by Police / 9.21.22
Iran (Frau Leben Freiheit /
Hadis Najafi / Erschossen von
der Polizei / 21.9.2022 Iran)
2023 DE Digitaldruck –
Digital print 100 × 70 cm
Donation Fons Matthias
Hickmann

106 Ñiko (*1941)
Photo: Alberto Korda (1928–2001)
Hasta la victoria siempre
(Auf zum Sieg, für immer –
Until Victory, Always)
1968 CU Siebdruck – Screenprint
98 × 55 cm

107 Jean-Claude Blanchard (*1945)
Mumia Abu-Jamal / 3 Juillet 82 /
17 aout 95 / 2 déc 99 / et mainte-
nant? (Mumia Abu-Jamal / 3. Juli
82 / 17. August 95 / 2. Dezember
99 / und wie geht's weiter? –
Mumia Abu-Jamal / July 3, 1982 /
August 17, 1995 / December 2,
1999 / And What's Next?)
1999 FR Siebdruck – Screenprint
102,5 × 67 cm
Donation Jean-Claude Blanchard

108 Paul Peter Piech (1920–1996)
I have a dream / I say to you today,
"Even though we face the
difficulties of today and tomorrow,
I still have a dream. (…) / Martin
Luther King, 1929–1968 (Ich habe
einen Traum / Ich sage euch
heute, dass ich immer noch einen
Traum habe, obwohl wir den
Schwierigkeiten von heute und
morgen entgegensehen. (…) /
Martin Luther King 1929–1968)
1983 US Hochdruck – Letterpress
64 × 45,5 cm

109 John Jennings (*1970)
Celebrate People's History /
To be black + conscious in America
is to live in a constant state of…
rage! James Baldwin (Feiert die
Geschichte des Volkes / Schwarz
und selbstbewusst zu sein in
Amerika bedeutet, in einem stän-
digen Zustand der Wut zu leben!
James Baldwin)
2015 US Offset 43,5 × 28 cm

110 Brett Colley (*1968)
Celebrate Peoples History! /
"I cannot stand and sing the
anthem. I cannot salute the flag;
I know that I am a Black man
in a white world. (…)" (Feiert die
Geschichte des Volkes!) / «Ich
kann nicht aufstehen und die Hym-
ne singen. Ich kann nicht vor
der Flagge salutieren. Ich weiss,
dass ich ein Schwarzer Mann
in einer weissen Welt bin. (…)»)
2020 US Offset 43,5 × 28 cm

111 Lana Grove
Celebrate People's History / Indi-
an Industrial Training School,
Haskell / Haskell Indian Nations
University began as the U.S.
Indian Industrial Training School.
It was one of the first Native
American boarding schools, estab-
lished in 1884, to remove Native
children from their families and as-
similate them into Eurocentric
culture. (…) (Feiert die Geschichte
des Volkes / Indian Industrial Training School Haskell / Die Haskell
Indian Nations University wurde
1884 unter dem Namen United
States Indian Industrial Training
School gegründet. Sie gehörte
zu den ersten Internatsschulen für
amerikanische Ureinwohnerin-
nen und Ureinwohnern, die das
Ziel verfolgten, die Kinder aus
ihren Familien zu lösen und ihre
Assimilation an die europäische
Kultur zu erreichen. (…))
2016 US Offset 43,5 × 28 cm

112 Roger Peet (*1973)
Men Against Sexism / 1977:
In Washington's maximum security Walla Walla Prison a group
of revolutionaries banded together
to break the culture of prison
rape and impunity and to imagine
a militant homosexuality in
opposition to all structures of domination. (…) (Männer gegen
Sexismus / 1977: Im Hochsicher-
heitsgefängnis von Walla Walla
im US-Bundesstaat Washington
schloss sich eine Gruppe von
Revolutionären zusammen, um
die Kultur der straffreien Verge-
waltigungen in Gefängnissen zu
durchbrechen und sich eine
militante, gegen alle Herrschafts-
strukturen gerichtete Homose-
xualität vorzustellen. (…))
2021 US Offset 43,5 × 28 cm

113 Colin Matthes (*1978)
Celebrate People's History /
Muhammad Ali / "Why should I
drop bombs and bullets on
Brown people in Vietnam while
so-called Negro people in
Louisville are treated like dogs?"
Muhammad Ali, 1967
(Feiert die Geschichte des Volkes /
Muhammad Ali / «Warum
sollte ich Bomben und Kugeln
auf braune Menschen in Vietnam
werfen, während sogenannte
N**** in Louisville wie Hunde
behandelt werden?»
Muhammad Ali 1967)
2004 US Offset 43,5 × 28 cm

114 Susie Wilson
Celebrate People's History / There
is nothing new under the sun,
but there are new suns. Octavia
E. Butler (Feiert die Geschichte
des Volkes / Es gibt nichts Neues
unter der Sonne, aber es gibt
neue Sonnen. Octavia E. Butler)
2019 US Offset 43,5 × 28 cm

115 Jenny Schmid (*1969)
Celebrate People's History / Int'l
Ladies' Garment Workers Union /
We'd Rather Starve Quick than
Starve Slow / The Great Revolt
1910 / 60,000 on Strike / The 1909
Uprising of 20,000 (Feiert die
Geschichte des Volkes / Internationale Gewerkschaft der Textil-
arbeiterinnen / Wir verhungern
lieber schnell als langsam / Der
grosse Aufstand von 1910 / 60 000
im Streik / Der Aufstand von
20 000 Menschen im Jahr 1909)
2019 US Offset 43,5 × 28 cm

116 Rocky Dobey (*1957)
Celebrate People's History /
Prison Justice Day / Started in
Canada in 1970 to Pay Tribute
to Prisoners who Died in Prison
(Feiert die Geschichte des Volkes /
Tag der Gerechtigkeit im Straf-
vollzug / Entstanden 1970 in Kana-
da zum Gedenken an Häftlinge,
die in Gefangenschaft starben)
2010, Entwurf – Design 2009
US Offset 43,5 × 28 cm

117 Josh MacPhee (*1973)
Celebrate Peoples' History /
Sacco / Vanzetti / Ferdinando
Nicola Sacco and Bartolomeo
Vanzetti were Italian-born
anarchists who arrived in the US
in 1908. Sacco was a shoe-maker
and Vanzetti a fish seller. (…)
(Feiert die Geschichte des Volkes /
Sacco / Vanzetti / Ferdinando
Nicola Sacco und Bartolomeo
Vanzetti waren in Italien geborene
Anarchisten, die 1908 in die USA
kamen. Sacco war Schuhmacher
und Vanzetti Fischverkäufer. (…))
2010 US Offset 43,5 × 28 cm

118 Jennifer Cartwright (*1979)
Celebrate Peoples History / ADAPT /
Since the early 80s, ADAPT
has been a national network of
activists with disabilities that
employs nonviolent civil disobe-
dience to demand changes in
policies that exclude people with
disabilities from American
society. (…) (Feiert die Geschichte
des Volkes / ADAPT / Seit den
frühen 1980er-Jahren ist ADAPT
ein nationales Netzwerk von
Aktivistinnen und Aktivisten mit
Behinderungen, das mit gewalt-
freiem zivilen Ungehorsam
Veränderungen in einer Politik
einfordert, die Menschen mit
Behinderungen aus der amerikanischen Gesellschaft aus-
schliesst. (…))
2006 US Offset 43,5 × 28 cm

119 Janet Attard (*1966)
Celebrate Peoples' History /
Major Taylor / Major Taylor
(1878–1932) was an African American cyclist who won the world
one mile track cycling champion-
ship in 1899. He set numerous
world records during his 30 years
of racing, and was the first
African American international
sports star. (…) (Feiert die
Geschichte des Volkes / Major
Taylor / Major Taylor (1878–1932)
war ein afroamerikanischer
Radrennfahrer, der 1899 die Welt-
meisterschaft im Bahnradfahren
über eine Meile gewann. In seiner
30-jährigen Radsportkarriere
stellte er zahlreiche Weltrekorde
auf und war der erste internationale afroamerikanische Sport-
star. (…))
2012 US Offset 43,5 × 28 cm

120 Shannon Gerard (*1973),
Mary Tremonte (*1978)
Celebrate People's History / Power
Up / Corita Kent was a radical
educator, silkscreen printing pop
artist, and activist agitator whose
pedagogical and political exuber-
ance extended to civil rights,
war resistance, feminist critique,
and a joyful participatory body
politic. (…) (Feiert die Geschichte
des Volkes / Power Up / Corita
Kent war eine radikale Pädagogin,
Siebdruck-Pop-Art-Künstlerin und
Aktivistin, deren pädagogische
und politische Bandbreite Bürgerrechte, Antikriegsaktivismus,
feministische Kritik und eine freud-
volle, partizipative Politik
umfasste. (…))
2017 US Offset 43,5 × 28 cm

121 Miriam Klein Stahl (*1971)
Celebrate People's History /
Funmilayo Ransome Kuti /
Francis Abigail Olufunmilayo
Thomas was born in Nigeria in
1900. Funmilayo (the name
she went by) was the first female
student at her elementary school
and then studied in England
before returning to Nigeria and
becoming a teacher. (…) (Feiert
die Geschichte des Volkes /
Funmilayo Ransome Kuti / Francis
Abigail Olufunmilayo Thomas
wurde 1900 in Nigeria geboren.
Funmilayo (wie sie genannt
wurde) war die erste weibliche
Schülerin an ihrer Grundschule
und studierte anschliessend
in England, bevor sie nach Nigeria
zurückkehrte und Lehrerin
wurde. (…))
2020 US Offset 43,5 × 28 cm

122 Tomie Arai (*1949)
Celebrate People's History!
Celebrar La Historia del Pueblo! /
Tenant Power! Save our Homes /
We Honor the History of New York
City Housing Rights Organizati-
ons: AAFE / The Brooklyn Anti-Gen-
trification Network / Brooklyn
Rent Strike Committee / Bronx Is
Not for Sale / (…) (Feiert die
Geschichte des Volkes! (…) / Alle
Macht den Mietern! Rettet unsere
Wohnungen! Wir würdigen die
Geschichte der Organisationen für
das Recht auf Wohnen: (…))
2021 US Offset 43,5 × 28 cm

123 John Jennings (*1970)
Celebrate Peoples History /
The Funsten 500 / St. Louis,
MO, 1933: 500 Black women who
worked as nutpickers for the
Funsten Nut Company mounted
a successful strike against the
industry giant, citing low wages
and inhumane working conditions
as major concerns. (…) (Feiert
die Geschichte des Volkes /
The Funsten 500 / St. Louis MO,
1933: 500 Schwarze Frauen,
die als Nussflückerinnen für die
Funsten Nut Company arbei-
teten, organisierten einen erfolgreichen Streik gegen den Bran-
chenriesen und führten niedrige
Löhne und unmenschliche
Arbeitsbedingungen als Haupt-
gründe an. (…))
2021 US Offset 43,5 × 28 cm

124 Eli Brown
Celebrate Peoples History /
Bayard Rustin / 1912–1987 / Loving
your enemy is manifest in put-
ting your arms not around the man
but around the social situation /
To take power from those who
misuse it, at which point they can
become human too. (Feiert die
Geschichte des Volkes / Bayard
Rustin / 1912–1987 / Seinen Feind
zu lieben bedeutet, nicht den
Menschen, sondern die gesellschaftliche Situation in die Arme
zu schliessen / Denjenigen die
Macht zu nehmen, die sie miss-
brauchen, damit auch sie wieder
zu Menschen werden können.)
2016 US Offset 43,5 × 28 cm

125 Camila Rosa (*1988)
Celebrate People's History /
Landless Workers' Movement /
With 1.5 million members,
the Movimento dos Trabalhadores
Sem Terra (MST), one of the
largest social movements in Latin
America. (…) (Feiert die Geschich-
te des Volkes / Bewegung der
Landarbeiter ohne Boden / Mit 1,5
Millionen Mitgliedern ist das
Movimento Dos Trabalhadores
Sem Terra (MST) eine der grössten
sozialen Bewegungen Latein-
amerikas. (…))
2020 US Offset 43,5 × 28 cm

126 Mincho Vega (*1979)
Celebrate People's History / Las
17+ / Beginning in 1999, women
in El Salvador have been charged
with aggravated homicide for
premature death in their wombs.
At least seventeen are known
internationally for receiving prison
sentences up to 50 years for
aggravated homicide. (…) (Feiert
die Geschichte des Volkes /
Las 17+ / Seit 1999 werden Frauen
in El Salvador wegen Mordes
angeklagt, weil ihr Kind im Mutter-
leib frühzeitig verstorben ist.
Mindestens 17 Frauen sind international bekannt, die wegen
Mordes zu Haftstrafen von bis zu
50 Jahren verurteilt wurden. (…))
2018 US Offset 43,5 × 28 cm

127 John Heartfield (1891–1968)
Adolf, der Übermensch:
Schluckt Gold und redet Blech
(Adolf the superman swallows
gold and spouts junk)
1932 (Nachdruck – Reprint 1976)
DE Offset 82 × 61 cm

128 Grapus, Les Graphistes Associés
[ohne Text – no text]
1990 FR Siebdruck – Screenprint
100 × 99,5 cm
Donation Les Graphistes
Associés, Paris

129 Anonym
Umweltschutz / Abrüstung
(Environmental Protection /
Disarmament)
1979 DE Offset 59,5 × 42 cm

130 Studio Flex /
Michael Speranza (*1993)
Brainwash (Gehirnwäsche)
2018 (Nachdruck – Reprint 2024)
CH Digitaldruck 128 × 89,5 cm
Donation Michael Speranza

131 Armando Milani (*1940)
I Am Not a Number
(Ich bin keine Nummer)
2008 (Nachdruck – Reprint 2024)
Diverse Erscheinungsländer –
Various countries of first appear-
ance Digitaldruck – Digital print
100 × 70 cm
Donation Armando Milani

132 Jean-Marc Seiler (1942–2024)
Du bist Kaufkraft
(You Have Purchasing Power)
1999 CH Digitaldruck –
Digital print 84 × 59,5 cm
Donation Jean-Marc Seiler

133 Lahav Halevy (*1965)
Her too. And her, and her, and
her, (…). All of them #MeToo
(Sie auch. Und sie, und sie, und
sie, (…). Sie alle #MeToo)
2017 Diverse Erscheinungsländer –
Various countries of first
appearance Offset 98 × 68 cm
Donation Lahav Halevy

134 Piär Amrein (*1957)
Put Out Putin!
(Werft Putin raus!)
2022 CH Hochdruck – Letterpress
35 × 50 cm
Donation Piär Amrein

135 Anna Berkenbusch (*1955)
Ich denke oft an den Krieg /
I Often Think about the War /
Unë mendoj shpesh për luftën
2003 DE Offset, Hochdruck –
Letterpress 119 × 84 cm
Donation Anna Berkenbusch

136 Studio AND /
Jean-Benoît Lévy (*1959)
Assalamu alaikom / Shalom
aleichem / La paix soit avec vous /
May Peace Be upon You /
Friede sei mit euch
2015 CH Siebdruck –
Screenprint 128 × 90 cm
Donation Jean-Benoît Lévy

137 Studio Kat Rahmani /
Golnar Kat Rahmani (*1983)
Woman Life Liberty /
#IranRevolution2022 /
#MahsaAmini (Frau Leben
Freiheit / #IranRevolution2022 /
#MahsaAmini)
2022 DE Siebdruck – Screenprint
59 × 42 cm
Donation Golnar Kat Rahmani

138 Frazier Dougherty (*1944),
Jon Hendricks (*1939),
Irving Petlin (1934–2018)
Photo: Ronald L. Haeberle (*1941)
Q. And Babies? A. And Babies.
(F: Und Babys? A: Und Babys.)
1970 US Offset 65 × 97 cm

139 Plazm / Joshua Berger (*1967)
Photo: Kim Kyung-Hoon (*1974)
Q. And Babies? A. And Babies.
(F: Und Babys? A: Und Babys.)
2018 US Digitaldruck –
Digital print 41,5 × 28 cm
Donation Joshua Berger

140 Yossi Lemel (*1957)
Photo: Eldad Cidor (*1971)
Israel Palestine 2002
2002 IL Siebdruck – Screenprint
180 × 119 cm
Donation Yossi Lemel

141 Paul Peter Piech (1920–1996)
Soweto
1977 US Hochdruck – Letterpress
91 × 58,5 cm
Donation Toppan Printing, Tokio

142 Anonym
Apartheid
ca. 1986 NL Offset 63 × 44,5 cm

143 Armando Milani (*1940)
Africa / The Forgotten Continent
(Afrika / Der vergessene Kontinent)
2007 (Nachdruck – Reprint 2024)
Diverse Erscheinungsländer –
Various countries of first appea-
rance Digitaldruck – Digital print
100 × 70 cm
Donation Armando Milani

144 Niklaus Troxler (*1947)
Capitalists of the World, Change!
(Kapitalisten aller Länder,
verändert euch!)
2019 CH Digitaldruck –
Digital print 128 × 91 cm
Donation Niklaus Troxler

145 Gladys Acosta Ávila (1941–2001)
Africa
1971 CU Offset 51 × 33 cm

146 David King (1943–2016)
Never Again! Stop the Nazi
National Front! (Nie wieder! Stoppt
die Nazis der National Front!)
1978 (Nachdruck – Reprint 1994)
JP Offset 73 × 51,5 cm
Donation Toppan Printing, Tokio

147 David King (1943–2016)
Amandla! Free the
Pretoria 12! (Amandla!
Lasst die Pretoria 12 frei!)
1978 GB Siebdruck – Screenprint
59,5 × 43 cm
Donation Richard Hollis

148 Luba Lukova (*1960)
War Crime (Kriegsverbrechen)
1999 US Siebdruck – Screenprint
87,5 × 64 cm
Donation Luba Lukova

149 Grapus
On va gagner! (Wir werden
gewinnen! – We Will Win!)
1991 FR Offset 80,5 × 60,5 cm
Donation François Chalet

150 Marlena Buczek Smith (*1977)
There Is No Victory in War
(Im Krieg gibt es keinen Sieg)
2011 US Giclée-Druck –
Giclée print 87 × 61 cm
Donation Marlena Buczek Smith

151 Fireworks Graphic Collective /
Terry Forman
Azania / We are not here to mourn
those who have died / Those
detained / Those banned / Those
imprisoned on Robben Island /
Whatever dirges we have had in
mind shall be transformed into
the war songs, battle hymns and
victory cries of all our black
heroes. (…) (Azania / Wir sind
nicht hier, um diejenigen zu
betrauern, die gestorben sind /
die verhaftet wurden / die
verboten wurden / die auf Robben Island interniert wurden /
Alle Klagelieder in unseren Köpfen
sollen in Kriegslieder, Kampfes-
hymnen und Siegesrufe all unserer
Schwarzen Helden verwandelt
werden. (…))
1985 US Siebdruck – Screenprint
57,5 × 36,5 cm

152 Herb Lubalin (1918–1981),
Christopher Blumrich (*1939)
The next war will determine not
what is right but what is left.
(Der nächste Krieg wird nicht
entscheiden, was richtig ist,
sondern was übrig bleibt.)
1972 (Nachdruck – Reprint 1994)
JP Offset 92,5 × 73 cm
Donation Printing Co. Ltd., Tokio

153 Jean Carlu (1900–1997)
Photo: André Vigneau
(1892–1968)
Pour le désarmement des nations
(Für die Abrüstung der Nationen –
For the Disarmament of Nations)
1932 FR Lithografie – Lithograph
157 × 115 cm

154 Mauro Bubbico (*1957)
Photo: Arnaldo Di Vittorio (*1969)
Migranti / Diritti e pace
(Migranten / Rechte und Frieden –
Migrants / Rights and Peace)
2011 IT Offset 97 × 67 cm
Donation Mauro Bubbico

155 Josep Renau (1907–1982)
¿Que haces tu para evitar esto?
Ayuda a Madrid (Was tust du,
um dies zu verhindern? Hilfe für
Madrid – What are you doing
to prevent this? Help for Madrid)
1937 ES Offset 80 × 56 cm
Donation Schweizerisches
Sozialarchiv, Zürich

156 Jānis Reinbergs (*1937)
Lūk, tava seja, Amerika!
(Schau, Dein Gesicht, Amerika! –
Look at Your Face, America!)
1972 SU Tiefdruck –
Gravure printing 90 × 59,5 cm

157 David Tartakover (*1944)
"It's sad when a child dies, and
hard as it is to say it, but he
was killed according to regula-
tions" / Childhood is not child's
play! («Es ist traurig, wenn
ein Kind stirbt, aber so schwer
es auch fällt, das zu sagen, er
wurde gemäss den Vorschriften
getötet» / Kindheit ist kein
Kinderspiel!)
1998 IL Offset 99 × 68,5 cm
Donation David Tartakover

158 John Heartfield (1891–1968)
Niemals wieder! (Never Again!)
1932 (Nachdruck – Reprint 1960)
DD Offset 57,5 × 41 cm

159 stettlerbros. /
Christoph Stettler (*1967)
Ukruine / Informationen auslas-
sen, weglassen, zurückhalten
(Ukruine / Omitting, Withholding,
Suppressing Information)
2015 CH Digitaldruck –
Digital print 128 × 90 cm
Donation Christoph Stettler

160 Atelier Bundi /
Stephan Bundi (*1950)
Stoppt die Folter. Amnesty
International (End Torture.
Amnesty International)
1985 (Nachdruck – Reprint 2005)
CH Siebdruck – Screenprint
128 × 90,5 cm
Donation Stephan Bundi

161 Nous Travaillons Ensemble, NTE /
Alex Jordan (*1947)
Kosovo / Timor / Tchétchénie
2001 FR Offset, Siebdruck –
Screenprint 80,5 × 60,5 cm
Donation Alex Jordan

162 Steff Geissbühler (*1942)
Peace (Frieden)
1985 US Offset 91,5 × 61 cm
Donation Steff Geissbühler

163 Peter Gee (1932–2005)
Say that I was a drum major /
Say that I was a drum major for
justice / Say that I was a drum
major for peace / Say that I was a
drum major for righteousness
(Sagt, ich sei ein Tambourmajor
gewesen / Sagt, ich sei ein
Tambourmajor der Gerechtigkeit
gewesen / Sagt, ich sei ein
Tambourmajor des Friedens
gewesen / Sagt, ich sei ein
Tambourmajor der Rechtschaf-
fenheit gewesen)
1968 US Siebdruck – Screenprint
76 × 48 cm

164 David Tartakover (*1944)
Photo: David Karp (1954–2024)
United Colors of Netanyahu.
1998 IL Offset 68,5 × 98 cm
Donation David Tartakover

165 The Martin Agency / Jerry Torchia
All those in favor of the death
penalty, raise your hand / Amnesty
International USA (Wer für die
Todesstrafe ist, hebe die Hand /
Amnesty International USA)
1992 US Offset 51 × 61 cm

166 Intégral Ruedi Baur et associés /
Ruedi Baur (*1956)
Peur de vos peurs
(Angst vor euren Ängsten –
Fear of Your Fears)
ca. 2000 FR Siebdruck –
Screenprint 77 × 59 cm
Donation Ruedi Baur

167 Anna Berkenbusch (*1955)
Like / Dislike
2011 DE Digitaldruck – Digital
print 119 × 84 cm
Donation Anna Berkenbusch

168 David Tartakover (*1944)
Frieden – Peace
2000 (Nachdruck – Reprint 2018)
IL Digitaldruck – Digital print
100 × 70 cm

169 Henryk Tomaszewski (1914–2005)
[ohne Text – no text]
1965 PL Offset 97 × 67 cm

170 Maciej Urbaniec (1925–2004)
A B C / a b c
1971 PL Offset 97,5 × 67,5 cm

171 Bruce Kaiper
Love / "Ideological Coverup"
(Liebe / «Ideologische
Vertuschung»)
1974 US Siebdruck – Screenprint
53,5 × 43,5 cm

Ausgewählte Literatur
Selected Bibliography

Amnesty International, Joanna Rippon, *The Art of Protest. A Visual History of Dissent and Resistance*, Woodbridge 2019.

ASARO, Mike Graham de La Rosa, Suzanne M. Schadl (eds.), *Getting Up for the People: The Visual Revolution of ASAR-Oaxaca*, Oakland 2014.

Bibliothèque de documentation internationale contemporaine, BDIC (ed.), *Internationales Graphiques, Collections d'affiches politiques, 1970–1990*, Paris 2016.

Bibliothèque de documentation internationale contemporaine, BDIC (ed.), *Affiche-Action, Quand la politique s'écrit dans la rue*, Paris 2013.

Bogerts, Lisa, *The Aesthetics of Rule and Resistance. Analyzing Political Street Art in Latin America*, New York 2022.

Breuer, Gerda, «Suffragetten: Frühes Corporate Design und Kommunikationsdesign in England / Suffragettes: Early Corporate and Communication Design in England», in: Gerda Breuer, *HerStories in Graphic Design. Dialoge, Kontinuitäten, Selbstermächtigungen. Grafikdesignerinnen 1880 bis heute / Dialogue, Continuity, Self-Empowerment. Women Graphic Designers from 1880 until Today*, Berlin 2023, pp. 102–113.

Coles, Anthony, *John Heartfield, Ein politisches Leben*, Köln / Weimar / Wien 2014.

Crettiez, Xavier, Pierre Piazza (eds.), *Iconographies rebelles. Sociologie des formes graphiques de contestation, Culture & Conflits*, no. 91/92, fall/winter 2013.

Döring, Jürgen, *Phantasie an die Macht. Politik im Künstlerplakat*, Hamburg 2011.

Frick, Richard, *Widerstand, Befreiung, Aufbau. Plakate und Fotografien als Zeitzeugnisse*, Zürich 2023.

Frick, Richard, *Das trikontinentale Solidaritätsplakat*, Bern 2003.

Glaser, Milton, Mirko Ilić, *The Design of Dissent*, Gloucester, MA 2005.

Goldstaub-Dainotto, Edna, «David Tartakover: The Imagery of Hope», in: *Graphis magazine*, vol. 53 (1997), no. 309, pp. 50–57.

HKS 13 (ed.), *Vorwärts bis zum Nieder mit. 30 Jahre Plakate unkontrollierter Bewegungen*, Berlin / Hamburg 2001.

HKS 13 (ed.), *Hoch die Kampf dem. 20 Jahre Plakate autonomer Bewegungen*, Berlin / Hamburg 1999.

Hoffmann, Tobias, Anna Grosskopf (eds.), *Das französische Grafikerkollektiv Grapus*, exhib. cat. Bröhan-Museum, Berlin 2018.

International Research Group on Authoritarianism and Counter-Strategies, kollektiv orangotango (eds.), *Beyond Molotovs. A Visual Handbook of Anti-Authoritarian Strategies*, Bielefeld 2024.

King, David, *Russian Revolutionary Posters. From Civil War to Socialist Realism, from Bolshevism to the End of Stalinism*, London 2015.

Lutz, Hans-Rudolf, Bruno Margadant (eds.), *Hoffnung und Widerstand. Das 20. Jahrhundert im Plakat der internationalen Arbeiter- und Friedensbewegung*, Zürich 1998.

MacPhee, Josh, *Celebrate People's History, The Poster Book of Resistance and Revolution*, New York 2020.

Massachusetts College of Art (ed.), *The Graphic Imperative. International Posters for Peace, Social Justice and the Environment, 1965–2005,* Boston 2005.

McQuiston, Liz, *Protest! A History of Social and Political Protest Graphics*, London 2019.

McQuiston, Liz, *Visual Impact. Creative Dissent in the 21st Century*, London 2015.

McQuiston, Liz, *Graphic Agitation 2. Social and Political Graphics in the Digital Age*, London 2004.

McQuiston, Liz, *Graphic Agitation. Social and Political Graphics since the Sixties*, London 1993.

Munro, Silas, *Strikethrough! Typographic Messages of Protest*, exhib. cat. Letterform Archive San Francisco, New York 2022.

Museum Folkwang, Deutsches Plakatmuseum (eds.), *Klaus Staeck, Sand im Getriebe*, Göttingen 2018.

Museum Ulm (ed.), *Protest! Gestalten. Von Otl Aicher bis heute*, Ulm 2023.

Radical Media Archive (ed.), *An Anthology of Counterculture and Political Graphic Design*, vol. 1, Paris 2024.

Richter, Bettina, «Ästhetik des Widerstands. Zur Visualisierung politischer Inhalte im Plakat», in: *Typografische Monatsblätter*, vol. 71 (2003), no. 5/6, pp. 2–9.

Rippon, Jo (ed.), *Rise Up! The Art of Protest*, Watertown 2020.

Rogger, Basil, Jonas Voegeli, Ruedi Widmer, Museum für Gestaltung Zürich (eds.), *Protest. Eine Zukunftspraxis*, Zürich 2018.

Whitley, Zoe, *The Graphic World of Paul Peter Piech*, London 2014.

Wlassikoff, Michel, *Mai 68, L'affiche en héritage*, Paris 2008.

www.anotherposterforpeace.org

www.davidkingdesigner.com/kings-work/political-posters

www.escuchamivoz.org/carteles-posters

www.mutzurwut.com

www.posterfortomorrow.org

Autorinnen und Autoren

Bettina Richter

Bettina Richter studierte Kunstgeschichte, Germanistik und Romanistik in Heidelberg, Paris und Zürich. 1996 promovierte sie über die Antikriegsgrafiken von Théophile-Alexandre Steinlen. Sie war von 1997 bis 2006 wissenschaftliche Mitarbeiterin, seit 2006 ist sie Kuratorin der Plakatsammlung des Museum für Gestaltung Zürich. In dieser Funktion realisierte sie unter anderem die Ausstellungen *Protest!* (2018) und *Talking Bodies* (2023). Von 2000 bis 2005 lehrte sie an der Zürcher Hochschule der Künste. Bettina Richter hat zahlreich publiziert und Vorträge zu kunst- und literaturhistorischen Themen sowie zum Plakat gehalten. Seit 2007 ist sie Herausgeberin der Reihe Poster Collection.

Lisa Bogerts

Lisa Bogerts studierte Politik- und Kommunikationswissenschaft sowie Friedens- und Konfliktforschung in Dresden, Magdeburg und Frankfurt am Main und promovierte 2019 über die Dialektik von ästhetischem Widerstand und Herrschaft in Lateinamerika. Von 2012 bis 2018 war sie wissenschaftliche Mitarbeiterin an verschiedenen Universitäten. Sie kuratierte von 2013 bis 2015 Ausstellungen zu politischer Street Art und Urban Art. 2017 verbrachte sie einen Forschungsaufenthalt an der New School for Social Research in New York. Seit 2018 forscht sie selbstständig und entwickelt Bildungsformate unter anderem zu künstlerischem Aktivismus im Exil, visueller Diskursanalyse, digitaler Bildsprache extrem rechter Bewegungen sowie zu Protestmobilisierung und sozialen Bewegungen.

Silas Munro

Silas Munro ist Designer, Künstler, Schriftsteller, Forscher, Kurator und Surfer und stammt vom Volk der Banyole in Ostuganda ab. Er gründete das Designstudio Polymode mit Sitz in Los Angeles und Raleigh. Munro ist Autor von *Strikethrough! Typographic Messages of Protest* und Kurator der gleichnamigen Ausstellung im Letterform Archive in San Francisco (2022–2023); ausserdem wirkte er an W. E. B. Du Bois' *Data Portraits. Visualizing Black America* (2018) mit und war 2021 Mitinitiator des ersten Kurses in Designgeschichte, der sich auf BIPoC-Menschen bezog: «Black Design in America: African Americans and the African Diaspora in Graphic Design 19th–21st Century». Seine gestalterischen und künstlerischen Werke wurden vielfach ausgestellt und sind in den Sammlungen verschiedener Institutionen vertreten. Munro ist Gründungsmitglied und ehemaliger Leiter des Masterstudiengangs Grafikdesign am Vermont College of Fine Arts.

ASARO

Die Asamblea de Artistas Revolucionarios de Oaxaca (ASARO) ist ein mexikanisches Kollektiv aus Künstlerinnen und Künstlern, das während der Proteste von 2006 entstanden ist. Mit Schablonen und Drucktechniken verwandeln ihre Mitglieder den öffentlichen Raum in eine Leinwand für Widerstand, Erinnerung und Gemeinschaft. Ihre anonyme, symbolische Kunst prangert Ungerechtigkeit an, dokumentiert Kämpfe und inspiriert durch kollektive, eindringliche und zutiefst politische visuelle Ausdrucksformen Bewegungen auf der ganzen Welt.

Authors

Bettina Richter

Bettina Richter studied art history as well as German and Romance languages and literature in Heidelberg, Paris, and Zurich, graduating in 1996 with a dissertation on the anti-war graphics of Théophile-Alexandre Steinlen. From 1997 to 2006, she served as a research associate at the Poster Collection of the Museum für Gestaltung Zürich and was appointed its curator in 2006. In this capacity she has realized, among other exhibitions, *Protest!* (2018) and *Talking Bodies* (2023). From 2000 to 2005, she taught at the Zurich University of the Arts. She has published and lectured extensively on subjects related to the history of art and literature, as well as on posters. Since 2007 she has served as the editor of the Poster Collection series.

Lisa Bogerts

Lisa Bogerts studied political science, communication studies, and peace and conflict studies in Dresden, Magdeburg, and Frankfurt am Main. From 2012 to 2018, she worked as a research assistant at various universities. From 2013 to 2015, she curated exhibitions on political street art and urban art, and in 2017, she was a visiting scholar at the New School for Social Research in New York City. In 2019, she completed a dissertation on the dialectics of aesthetic rule and resistance in Latin America. Since 2018, she has pursued independent research and educational projects on topics such as artistic activism in exile, visual discourse analysis, the digital imagery of extreme right-wing movements, protest mobilization, and social movements.

Silas Munro

Silas Munro is a designer, artist, writer, researcher, curator, and surfer. He is a descendant of the Banyole people of eastern Uganda. He founded the design studio Polymode, based in Los Angeles and Raleigh. Munro is the author of *Strikethrough! Typographic Messages of Protest* and curator of the exhibition of the same name at Letterform Archive (2022–23). He was a contributor to W. E. B. Du Bois's *Data Portraits: Visualizing Black America* (2018) and co-authored the first BIPOC-centered design history course, Black Design in America: African Americans and the African Diaspora in Graphic Design 19th–21st Century (2021). His designs and visual art have been exhibited widely and are represented in the collections of various institutions. Munro is Founding Faculty and Chair Emeritus of the MFA Program in Graphic Design at Vermont College of Fine Arts.

ASARO

The Asamblea de Artistas Revolucionarios de Oaxaca (ASARO) is a Mexican artists' collective that emerged during the 2006 protests. Using stencils and printmaking, its members transform public space into a canvas for resistance, memory, and community. Their anonymous, symbolic art challenges injustice, documents struggles, and inspires global movements through urgent and deeply political collective visual expression.

Back issues of the Poster Collection

www.lars-mueller-publishers.com

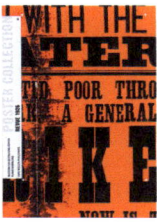
01

02

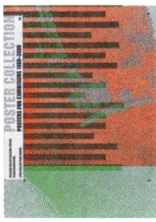
03

04

05

06

07

08

09

10

11

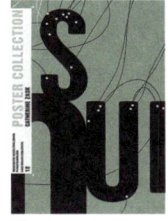
12

13

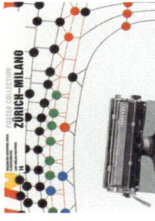
14

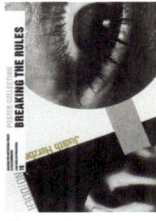
15

16

17

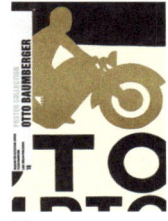
18

19

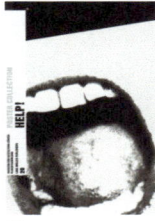
20

21

22

23

24

25

26

27

28

29

30

31

32

33

34

35

36

Dank

Publikations- und Ausstellungsprojekte sind immer ein willkommener Anlass, den eigenen umfangreichen Bestand an Plakaten themenspezifisch zu sichten, aufzuarbeiten und zu ergänzen. Für die vorliegende Publikation konnten wir auf zahlreiche Protest- und Widerstandsplakate im Archivbestand zurückgreifen, bilden sie doch seit vielen Jahren einen wichtigen Sammlungsschwerpunkt. Nicht wenige der historischen Plakate stammen aus der vom Museum erworbenen einzigartigen Sammlung von Bruno Margadant (1929–2013), der über Jahre hinweg Plakate zu weltweiten Kämpfen von Arbeiter-, Revolutions- und Protestbewegungen zusammengetragen hat. Viele Plakate der jüngeren Zeit wurden der Plakatsammlung von Gestalterinnen und Gestaltern geschenkt, oft in direkter Reaktion auf aktuelle politische Ereignisse, die damit dokumentiert werden. Für diese grosszügigen Donationen bedanken wir uns herzlich.

Acknowledgments

Publication and exhibition projects are always a welcome opportunity to explore our own extensive inventory of posters with an eye toward specific subjects and to supplement these with new works. For this publication, we were able to draw on numerous protest and resistance posters in our archives, as they have been an important focus of the collection for many years. Quite a few of the historical posters come from the unique collection of Bruno Margadant (1929–2013), which the museum acquired in 1997. For many years, Margadent collected posters focused on labor struggles around the world, protests, and revolutionary movements. Many recent posters have been donated to the Poster Collection by their designers, often in direct response to the contemporary political events they document. We would like to express our sincere thanks for these generous gifts.

Museum für Gestaltung Zürich

Eine Publikation des Museum für Gestaltung Zürich
Christian Brändle, Direktor

A Publication of the Museum für Gestaltung Zürich
Christian Brändle, Director

Resist!
Konzept und Redaktion / Concept and editing:
Bettina Richter, Petra Schmid, Alessia Contin
Gestaltung / Design: Teo Schifferli
Satz / Typesetting: Lars Müller Publishers
Übersetzung / Translation: Helen Ferguson (Ger.–Eng.),
Antoinette Aichele-Platen (Eng.–Ger.)
Lektorat und Korrektorat Deutsch / German copyediting
and proofreading: Markus Zehentbauer
Lektorat und Korrektorat Englisch / English copyediting
and proofreading: Adam Blauhut
Fotografie / Photography: Ivan Šuta
Bildrechte / Image rights: Regula Kreis
Lithografie / Repro: prints professional, Berlin, Germany
Druck und Einband / Printing and binding:
Printer Trento s.p.a., Trento, Italy

Reihe / Series «Poster Collection»
Herausgegeben von / Edited by
Museum für Gestaltung Zürich, Plakatsammlung
Bettina Richter, Kuratorin der Plakatsammlung /
Curator of the Poster Collection
In Zusammenarbeit mit / In cooperation with
Petra Schmid, Leiterin Publikationen / Head of Publications

© 2025
Zürcher Hochschule der Künste
und Lars Müller Publishers

Z The museum of
Zurich University of the Arts
zhdk.ch

Museum für Gestaltung Zürich
Ausstellungsstrasse 60
Postfach
8031 Zurich, Switzerland
www.museum-gestaltung.ch

Museum für Gestaltung Zürich
Plakatsammlung / Poster Collection
sammlung@museum-gestaltung.ch

Lars Müller Publishers
Pfingstweidstrasse 6
8005 Zurich, Switzerland
www.lars-mueller-publishers.com
+41 44 274 37 40

Produktsicherheit / Product safety
Hersteller / Producer: Lars Müller Publishers GmbH
Verantwortliche Person gemäss EU-Verordnung
2023/988 (GPSR) / Responsible person in accordance
with EU Regulation 2023/988 (GPSR):
Michael Klein, Verlagsvertretung / Sales representative
Hub 1, DE-84149 Velden
+49 8742 964 552 2, gpsr@lars-mueller-publishers.com

ISBN 978-3-03778-795-3

Printed in Italy

Wir danken für Unterstützung /
For their support we thank:

.:::: APG|SGA